# Estefan
# Kitchen

# ESTEFAN
## KITCHEN

EMILIO & GLORIA ESTEFAN

celebra

Celebra
Published by New American Library, a division of
Penguin Group (USA) Inc., 375 Hudson Street,
New York, New York 10014, USA
Penguin Group (Canada), 90 Eglinton Avenue East, Suite 700, Toronto,
Ontario M4P 2Y3, Canada (a division of Pearson Penguin Canada Inc.)
Penguin Books Ltd., 80 Strand, London WC2R 0RL, England
Penguin Ireland, 25 St. Stephen's Green, Dublin 2,
Ireland (a division of Penguin Books Ltd.)
Penguin Group (Australia), 250 Camberwell Road, Camberwell, Victoria 3124,
Australia (a division of Pearson Australia Group Pty. Ltd.)
Penguin Books India Pvt. Ltd., 11 Community Centre, Panchsheel Park,
New Delhi - 110 017, India
Penguin Group (NZ), 67 Apollo Drive, Rosedale, North Shore 0632,
New Zealand (a division of Pearson New Zealand Ltd.)
Penguin Books (South Africa) (Pty.) Ltd., 24 Sturdee Avenue,
Rosebank, Johannesburg 2196, South Africa

Penguin Books Ltd., Registered Offices:
80 Strand, London WC2R 0RL, England

First published by Celebra,
a division of Penguin Group (USA) Inc.

First Printing, November 2008
10 9 8 7 6 5 4 3 2 1

Copyright © Estefan Enterprises, Inc., 2008
All rights reserved

Photographs courtesy of Moris Moreno Photography, except photographs on pages 2, 6, 10, 46, 70, 132, 162, 184,
and 212 courtesy of the Estefan Family Archives.

CELEBRA and logo are trademarks of Penguin Group (USA) Inc.

LIBRARY OF CONGRESS CATALOGING-IN-PUBLICATION DATA:
Estefan, Emilio.
  Estefan kitchen/Emilio Estefan, Gloria Estefan.
    p. cm.
  ISBN 978-0-451-22518-4
  1. Cookery, Cuban.  2. Food habits—Cuba.  I. Estefan, Gloria.  II. Title.
  TX716.C8E74 2008
  641.597291—dc22          2008006765

Set in Whitman
Designed by Pauline Neuwirth, Neuwirth & Associates, Inc.

PUBLISHER'S NOTE
The recipes contained in this book are to be followed exactly as written. The publisher is not responsible for your
specific health or allergy needs that may require medical supervision. The publisher is not responsible for any adverse
reactions to the recipes contained in this book.
    The publisher does not have any control over and does not assume any responsibility for author or third-party
Web sites or their content.

*To Consuelo, Nena and Mama Gloria,*
*who nurtured us with lots of love and food . . .*

# Contents

———⚍———

## SIDES

## SANDWICHES

## DESSERTS

## BEVERAGES

# Estefan Kitchen

GLORIA'S GRANDPARENTS CONSUELO
AND LEONARDO GARCIA

# Introduction

GLORIA ESTEFAN

———◦∞◦———

THEY SAY THAT music is the way to a person's soul and food is the way to a person's heart.

Although people know me for my music, I actually come from a long line of chefs on both sides of my family. Cuban cooking was at the center of my culture right from the beginning.

My great-grandfather, my grandmother Consuelo's father, was renowned for his cooking, and he served as the personal chef for two presidents in Cuba. His daughter, my grandmother Consuelo, was also an amazing cook. She left Cuba with my grandfather when she was fifty-six years old. At that time, the Cuban government would not allow anyone out of the country with any personal possessions. Even though they arrived in the United States with empty pockets, they were filled with integrity, determination, and hope. So she told my grandfather: "I've got an idea. If it works we're going to be okay. And if it doesn't, then we're going to be living under a bridge."

Her feeling was that if you do what you love, people will love what you do. And her love was cooking.

She had rented a house that had its backyard facing a park in Miami where Little League games were held. One day, she decided to make *croquetas*, tamales, and *pan con lechón* sandwiches—all foods that would travel well and that she could put in a shopping cart. She walked the cart over to the park and the very first day, she sold out of all the items she had brought. Just like that, her cooking became her livelihood. Her entrepreneurship paid off. Before long, she was earning about $5,000 each weekend—a very successful home business for the 1960s.

As her business grew more successful over time, she began to offer catering services for weddings, *quinceañeras* (sweet fifteen parties) and other occasions for her customers and friends. Despite the growing business, she continued to do all the cooking herself. I lived with my grandma Consuelo, so I would spend my entire day in the kitchen with my *abuela*, helping her and watching her cook. And even today, some of my most treasured memories are of the days I spent with her.

My grandmother loved to feed me—she made it her mission. From her point of view, I was too skinny as a child. I was really just a normal-sized kid, but to Cubans normal is still considered "skinny." She would do anything to get me to eat more. We would start eating at the kitchen table and she would give me my last mouthful of food sitting on the butcher's counter three blocks away. She couldn't stop feeding me. She would say, "Okay, now one more" and "Another one" and so on. It was so important to her that I eat.

This constant feeding frenzy continued throughout my upbringing. She was constantly trying to feed me and make things that I would like. Although, I have to confess, I'm not a martyr. I loved everything she made! There was so much love in her cooking that today, for me, love and food are completely intertwined.

I don't have a single memory of my grandmother Consuelo where she's not cooking. For her, cooking was her life and her art and it sustained her family in every way.

My grandfather, on my father's side of the family, was also an amazing and very successful cook. He actually managed one of the first Cuban restaurants in Miami, Salon Tropical. I remember watching him as he would come over to my parents' house and cook for us.

From those experiences and influences early in my life, I've never really needed to cook from a recipe. Like my grandmother, I'm resourceful. I can prepare a meal with virtually any ingredients I find in the fridge.

My grandmother's dream was always to open a restaurant. When my grandfather passed away, she had to run the catering business on her own. She was resilient and managed to do well, yet her dream of having her own restaurant never materialized.

Many years later, after Emilio and I achieved success with our music, an opportunity came along to open a Cuban restaurant on Miami Beach. Emilio and I really felt it was a great extension of what we had already accomplished through our music, which was to showcase our culture to the world. It was another way to show our fans who we are—not just through our music, but through our culinary heritage.

The restaurants brought those two worlds together for us. When you walk into any one of our restaurants, you're surrounded by Cuban music while you eat. So it's food *and* music, two of the best things in life. For us, it was just a very natural progression. And for me there was the added value of making my grandma's dream come true. Although my grandmother Consuelo was no longer with us, it was always something that I wanted to do for our culture, but mostly for her.

Our restaurants allow people from all over the world to discover Cuban food, and learn more about our culture and our heritage. And very often they're surprised by the food. Generally speaking, people think that Cuban food is very spicy, and it's not that way at all. We marinate a lot, so the dishes are very tasty and richly flavored, but not very spicy.

Here, in this book, we hope to share our culture and our food with you. Those who are fans of our restaurants will be able to cook at home the dishes they love. And those who haven't made it to one of our restaurants yet can still enjoy the great foods we make there, and at our home.

We are honored to share them with you the way my grandmother did—with love.

EMILIO'S PARENTS, CARMEN "NENA"
AND EMILIO "CAPE" ESTEFAN

# *Introduction*

EMILIO ESTEFAN

—⟨∞∞⟩—

TRULY BELIEVE THAT the land in which you are born leaves a permanent impression on your soul. Your birthplace transcends geography and becomes your culture. My culture lives in my heart and mind.

Certain flavors and smells stay in your memory, reaching as far back as your childhood. I lived in Santiago, at the far eastern end of Cuba, until I was thirteen years old. And whenever I smell or taste Cuban cooking, it reminds me of that time and brings back memories of family and of my childhood.

For Cubans, food is a celebration, not just during holidays, but every time we sit and share a meal with family and friends. For us, food goes far, far beyond simple nutrition. It's about heritage, culture, and tradition.

I've been lucky to have traveled around the world, and I love much of the cuisine it has to offer. I love Lebanese food—as I am part Lebanese—Italian food, and Spanish food, but the food I love more than any other is traditional Cuban food—*comida criolla*, as we call it. It's my favorite because of how simple it is. Generally, the seasonings are based on garlic, lime or bitter orange, and onion. We use that simple blend as a marinade, or mix them together and sauté them to make the *sofrito*, which is the heart of so many of our dishes.

Cuban food is a part of who I am. It connects me to my past, and helps to keep the traditions alive for my children. I want them to know what I have enjoyed since my childhood and to create their own memories when they smell the sweet aroma of *arróz con leche* or the strong smell of Cuban coffee brewing.

Gloria and I have been very lucky to live the American Dream, especially for two people who left Cuba with nothing. Our cultural roots are very important to us, and we've never forgotten where we came from. We've actually made it our mission to share our culture and traditions not only with our family, but with the world as well. We did it first with our music and then, when we had the chance, we did it with our restaurants. Our restaurants are a way to invite people to our table, to give them a taste of the dishes we grew up with, the ones we still enjoy and share with our family and friends.

The success of our restaurants has been proof that people love traditional Cuban food as much as we do. Our Bongos Cuban Café in Walt Disney World, Orlando, is more than a restaurant; it's a historic landmark as it places Cuban food front and center among American cuisines. It's a tribute to our parents, who gave us so much and worked so hard so that we would have opportunities here. And it's a celebration of the heritage they wanted us to be proud of. Bongos Cuban Café is a living testament to the fact that we will never forget Cuba, our parents, or our families. To me, it's an incredible opportunity to share our culture, and to maintain a piece of our homeland outside of Cuba.

Our very first restaurant, Larios on the Beach, opened in 1992 on Miami Beach's famous Ocean Drive. It is now under our Bongos Cuban Café brand and is one of the most popular restaurants on South Beach.

Bongos Cuban Café was one of the first restaurants to open in downtown Disney, and now, ten years later, it continues to be one of the leading restaurants at Walt Disney World, the most "American" place on earth. The menu is our typical Cuban food, *comida criolla*. But it's been a hit with people from all over the world, who come and try the food and fall in love with our style of cooking. The popularity of Bongos Cuban Café at Disney led us to open another location in Miami, and, most recently, in Puerto Vallarta, Mexico, and at Miami International Airport.

The motivation to share our food and our culture with everyone, just as we have with our music, is what inspired us to write this book. We're opening our kitchen for the very first time and sharing our recipes and our techniques, so that you can create the traditional tastes of Cuba at home! These are the recipes from our homeland, from our families, and from our hearts.

*¡Que siga la tradicion!*

# Appetizers

GLORIA COOKING WITH HER DAUGHTER, EMILY

$\mathcal{M}$OST OF THE appetizers we've included here are dishes that are served at our restaurants. They're also some of the most basic foods in Cuban culture. They're things that I watched my grandmother make throughout my life.

Just because we call them appetizers, though, doesn't mean you can *only* serve them before a meal. As a matter of fact, if you eat a full serving of these appetizers, you're not going to have a lot of room for dinner. (We Cubans, we'll make room, no matter what . . .)

Generally, when we get together with family and friends, there's lots of music and lots of finger food like this to go around. All of these appetizers are perfect for gatherings, small or large. People can grab them, pop them in their mouths, and get back to dancing, which is really why we get together in the first place.

They can also be served as Cuban tapas, and let people sample and share different dishes and of course, you can also serve these dishes as the main courses. Often enough, we'll serve *masitas de puerco,* the fried pork chunks, as a meal. Serve a few hefty cubes of this meat along with some rice, beans, and *plátanos maduros* or *tostones,* and you've got a full Cuban meal.

The same is true of the *croquetas de jamón.* It's an all-around food that works as an appetizer, a snack, or a meal. Ham croquettes get served alone or with crackers for breakfast or lunch, as bite-sized party snacks, and with rice, beans, and *yuca* or plantains for dinner. We'll even put them in a sandwich.

As you'll probably notice, there's not a lot of salads or vegetables in Cuban cuisine. The only vegetables, pretty much, are the plantain—which we love—*yuca* (cassava) and *malanga*. It's really a Caribbean cooking style, relying on the things that grow in the islands.

Some of the dishes are similar to foods in other cultures. For example, whenever I'm going to introduce *papa rellena* to any of my friends, and they ask me what it is, I tell them, "It's a Cuban knish." It's mashed potatoes stuffed with meat, and then breaded and fried.

Cuban cooking, though had influences from many different cultures. A lot of ideas came from Spain because the Spaniards were the last settlers in Cuba and ruled the island for so long. But Cuba had a lot of mixes, including French, English, Chinese. And the Africans, needless to say, were very large contributors to our culture.

Out of all those influences, we developed our own cuisine, and these appetizers offer a variety of examples.

*—Gloria*

MASITAS DE PUERCO

# Masitas de Puerco

### (CUBAN-STYLE FRIED PORK CHUNKS)

꧁꧂

Masitas de puerco, *fried pork chunks, is a typical Cuban dish, born in the island's countryside. After the people made pork, they would leave chunks of the pork marinating overnight. When they went to reheat the pork the following day, it was already saturated with flavor. That's how they made fried pork chunks.*

*One of the great things about* masitas de puerco *is that they serve many purposes. Often enough, we'll serve them as a main course, along with some* tostones *or* platanos maduros *and rice and beans. For parties you can cut them into bite-sized pieces, stick toothpicks in them, and offer them as hors d'oeuvres.*

—Emilio

꧁꧂

## YIELD: 4 TO 6 SERVINGS

2 cups *mojo* (see recipe on page 159)

3 lbs of pork loin

pinch of cumin powder

2 bay leaves

1/3 cup vegetable oil

1 medium onion, peeled and thinly sliced

1. Prepare the *mojo*.

2. Cube pork into 1" × 1" × 1" cubes and place into a large roasting pan.

3. In a small bowl, whisk the cumin into the *mojo*, then pour the mixture over the pork chunks, and add the bay leaves and cover with plastic wrap. Place the pan in the refrigerator and let the pork marinate overnight.

4.  Remove pork from refrigerator and heat oil to 350°F over medium-high heat. Then, using a slotted spoon and allowing excess marinade to drain into the pan, remove the pork from the *mojo* and fry for about 10 minutes, turning once about halfway through, until the pork is brown and crisped. Then add the onions and sauté for about 3 minutes, until the onions are translucent.

5.  Transfer to a serving platter and serve hot.

# Papas Rellenas

(BREADED MASHED POTATOES STUFFED WITH GROUND BEEF CREOLE)

⚬⚬⚬

Papas rellenas *are one of my daughter's favorite foods. She's loved them ever since she was a little baby. Nobody makes them as good as my grandmother did, but these come pretty close.*

*Whenever I see a papa rellena, I see my grandmother's hand cupping the mashed potatoes and forming them into a ball. I can see the whole process in front of me: how she filled the half-sphere with ground beef and covered the meat with more potatoes. Then she coated the whole thing with breading and fried it in oil.*

*The finished product is basically a "Cuban knish." That's what I tell my non-Cuban friends. The difference is the seasoning.*

*If you're counting calories, I wouldn't eat them every day. But you can serve them as an appetizer, or for breakfast, the way we sometimes do.*

—Gloria

⚬⚬⚬

## YIELD: 16 TO 20 STUFFED POTATOES

picadillo (see recipe on page 87)

6 large russet potatoes

a pinch of salt, for boiling the potatoes

1/2 tsp salt

2 cloves garlic, minced

1 jar of pimento-stuffed olives

4 eggs

1 cup *galleta molida* (can substitute with unseasoned bread crumbs)

1/4 cup all-purpose flour

vegetable oil for frying

1.   Make the *picadillo* and let cool.

2. Peel the potatoes, cut them into cubes, and put them into a medium-sized pot. Cover them with water and add a pinch of salt. Bring the potatoes to a boil over high heat, then reduce heat to medium and simmer until tender (approximately 20 minutes). Drain the potatoes and place them back into pot and shake the pot over the stove for about a minute to allow any excess moisture to evaporate. Transfer the potatoes to a large mixing bowl. Then add salt and garlic to taste. Mash the potatoes using a masher or ricer and let them cool completely.

3. Place wax paper on two large baking sheets.

4. Using an ice-cream scooper, take a large scoop of the potato mash, then split it into two semi-spheres. Mold each semi-sphere into a small bowl, using your fingers. Fill one of the halves (just to the rim of bowl) with *picadillo.* Fill the other half about ¾ full, then stuff an olive into this half, allowing the olive to protrude a bit. Combine the two halves to make a sphere, pinching at the seams to ensure that they don't come apart while cooking. Then smooth them with your palms. Repeat with the remaining mashed potatoes and *picadillo,* placing the prepared *papas rellenas* on one of the baking sheets.

5. Whisk the eggs in a large bowl. Combine the *galleta molida* and flour in another large bowl. Dip the stuffed potato into the beaten eggs in batches of about four. Drain any excess by placing the potatoes into a strainer placed over the bowl containing the eggs. Then dredge the moistened stuffed potatoes in the flour mixture, making sure all sides are covered.

6. Place the breaded *papas rellenas* onto the second baking sheet and cover them with plastic wrap. Place the tray in the refrigerator for 3 to 4 hours.

### Tip from the Kitchen

The prepared *papas rellenas* can be frozen overnight or for a few days. Do not thaw before frying, but vary cooking time as necessary to ensure the *papas rellenas* are completely cooked.

PAPAS RELLENAS

7. Fill a large skillet with vegetable oil, just deep enough to cover about half of a *papa rellena*, and heat over medium-high heat to 360°F.

8. Using a slotted spoon, carefully place the *papas rellenas* in the heated oil and fry for about 4 or 5 minutes until golden brown on all sides, turning over once about halfway through.

### Tip from the Kitchen

At our restaurants, our chefs fry the *papas rellenas* in a deep fryer, and if you have one, we recommend using it because it will ensure a uniform color. If you use a deep fryer, heat the vegetable oil to 375°F and place a single row of prepared *papas rellenas* in the basket; then immerse the basket in the fryer. Cook for 3 to 4 minutes, until golden brown.

9. Let the *papas rellenas* cool for 8 to 10 minutes on a plate lined with paper towels to absorb excess oil. Transfer them to a serving dish and serve at once.

# Mariquitas

———✺———

These are often considered "Cuban potato chips." You can slice them the same way you would slice a banana to put on cereal, at a slight angle to make the slivers a little longer, or you can cut them lengthwise into long strips. Just cut them thin, about the same width you would for potato chips. (You can actually find plantain chips in the potato chip aisle at a lot of grocery stores, but they won't be the same as when they are homemade.)

This recipe is more proof of just how versatile plantains are, and how many ways we've found to include them in Cuban cuisine.

To add some extra flavor, serve them with some mojo in a little bowl so people can dip them. You don't want to pour the mojo over the mariquitas, because then it will make the plaintain chips soggy. It's best to dip. The mojo is very garlicky, but it's delicious. Just make sure everybody eats the garlic so you can talk to each other.

—Gloria

———✺———

**YIELD: 6 TO 8 SERVINGS**

4 large green plantains

vegetable oil

salt

½ cup *mojo*, served on the side for dipping (see recipe on page 159)

MARIQUITAS

1. Peel the plantains. Using a vegetable peeler or mandolin, finely slice the plantains (about the width you would slice potatoes for potato chips). You can slice the plantains lengthwise or crosswise, as you prefer.

> **Tip from the Kitchen**
>
> Slicing the chips lengthwise enables you to use them to create "plantain chip sculptures" in your favorite Cuban dish, by carefully inserting two or three chips—upright and placed so they rest on one another at the top—into your main course or side dish to give your dish some tasty height.

2. Fill a large skillet with enough vegetable oil to completely cover plantain chips. Then heat the vegetable oil to 360°F.

3. Fry the plantain chips in batches, placing the chips in the heated oil carefully so as not to get splattered. Do not overfill the pan, as the chips will stick to one another. Turn the chips occasionally and fry until browned on both sides, about 5 to 7 minutes. Be careful not to overcook them.

4. Remove the chips from the oil and place them on a plate lined with paper towels to absorb excess oil. Wait a few minutes. Then salt to taste and transfer to a serving dish.

5. While cooking the remaining batches, keep the fried chips warm by placing them in the oven at 170°F until ready to serve.

6. Serve with *mojo* on the side for dipping.

YUCA FRITA

# Yuca Frita

### (CASSAVA FRIES)

⸿

Yuca frita *is our version of steak fries. But we use* yuca *instead of potatoes.*

*Your grocer may know* yuca *better as cassava, depending on where you live. But* yuca *is a very starchy vegetable that the Spaniards found growing in Cuba when they arrived on the island.*

*Boiled* yuca *is one of the things that we commonly serve as part of* Noche Buena, *our traditional Christmas Eve feast, and this recipe is a great way to turn the leftovers into something fresh. They're a great alternative to french fries.*

*All you have to do is slice the boiled* yuca *into fat wedges and fry them up the same way you would steak fries. The result is delicious and a great change from potatoes. It's just a different taste altogether.*

*—Gloria*

⸿

**YIELD: 4 SERVINGS**

2 lbs *yuca*

6 cups water (more or less)

3 tsp salt

vegetable oil

1/2 cup of *mojo*, served on the side for dipping (see recipe on page 159)

1. Peel and thoroughly wash the *yuca*. Cut it into wedges approximately 1" × 3" × ½" **(Note: Wedges should be about the size of steak fries, but each wedge will be a different size; these measurements are intended merely as a guideline.)** Pour the water and salt into a large saucepan and bring the water to a boil. Add the *yuca* wedges and bring the water to a boil a second time. Then reduce heat to low and

cook, uncovered, for approximately 12 to 15 minutes or until the *yuca* is just tender.

2. Remove the *yuca* wedges from the water and place them in a colander to drain excess water. Then remove them to a plate and pat dry with paper towels or with a kitchen towel.

3. Fill a large skillet with enough vegetable oil to completely cover the *yuca* wedges (if placed in a single layer). Then heat the vegetable oil to 360°F. Important: Do *not* immerse the yuca until the oil has reached the appropriate frying temperature.

4. Once the oil is properly heated, place the wedges into the heated oil carefully so as not to get splattered. Fry them until deep golden brown on both sides, about 6 to 8 minutes.

5. Remove the *yuca* from the oil using a slotted spoon and transfer the wedges to a plate lined with paper towels to absorb excess oil. Wait a few minutes, and then salt to taste before serving.

6. If you need to fry in batches, or if the rest of your meal is not cooked, the fried *yuca* wedges may be kept warm by placing them in the oven at 170°F until ready to serve.

CROQUETAS DE JAMÓN

# Croquetas de Jamón

### (HAM CROQUETTES)

———— ✺ ————

Croquetas *are great-tasting treats that we eat for breakfast, lunch, dinner, and as finger food at parties. So they are very, very versatile. They're also an amazing way to extend your food dollar by turning your leftovers into a delicious new meal.*

*The most common ones, and the ones we make at the restaurants, are ham, but you can make them out of almost anything. Regardless of what part of the meat you have left over, you can grind it up and make* croquetas.

*My favorite* croquetas *that my grandmother made were codfish* croquetas. *But you can also make them from chicken, turkey, beef—you name it.*

—Gloria

———— ✺ ————

## YIELD: 20 TO 24 CROQUETAS

2 tbsp white onion, minced

1 clove garlic, minced

6 tbsp (¾ stick) butter

½ cup plus 1 tbsp all-purpose flour, sifted

¾ cup whole milk

salt

ground white pepper

1 tsp *vino seco*

1 ½ cups (1 lb) ground smoked ham (or ground cooked chicken, turkey, pork, or beef)

2 cups cracker meal (*galleta molida*)

6 large eggs

corn, vegetable, or canola, oil, for frying

3 limes, sliced into wedges

saltine crackers

1. Process the minced onion and garlic in a minichop or blender.

2. Heat butter in a heavy-bottomed saucepan over medium heat, and then reduce temperature to low and add onion and garlic purée. Sauté for about 4 to 5 minutes, until just before the purée browns. Add the flour, about ¼ cup at a time, mixing well with a wooden spoon after each addition.

3. Stir in the milk and cook over low heat for 2 to 3 minutes, stirring constantly with a wooden spoon, until the béchamel has thickened and you can see the bottom of the pan when you stir. Remove from heat and stir in the salt (to taste) and white pepper (to taste), *vino seco* and ground ham (or other cooked, ground poultry or meat), then return the pan to low heat and cook for an additional 4 to 5 minutes, stirring frequently.

> ### Tip from the Kitchen
>
> *Vino* seco is a dry white cooking wine commonly found in Latin markets or the Latin food aisle of your local grocery. You may substitute dry white wine if your market doesn't carry *vino seco*.

4. Transfer the ham filling into a bowl and let cool to room temperature. Cover the bowl with plastic wrap or waxed paper and refrigerate overnight or for at least 3 hours.

5. Place the cracker meal into a large bowl. In another large bowl, beat the eggs.

6. Remove the ham filling from the refrigerator and place into a pastry piping bag (or a resealable plastic bag, then cut a corner off) with an opening of ¾ inch to 1 inch in diameter, pipe the mixture onto a cookie sheet lined with parchment paper, forming croquettes about 2½ inches to 3 inches long. (You can also form the croquettes using your hands, which should be lightly floured, but piping ensures a uniform appearance. You can also make smaller croquettes, about ¾ inch thick and 2½ inches long.) The rolled croquettes should have the shape of short hot dogs (see photograph).

7. Dip the formed croquettes into the beaten eggs, covering all sides and both ends. Remove each croquette from the bowl, allow excess eggs to drip off, then dredge in cracker meal, again making sure to cover all sides and both ends in the cracker mixture. Set breaded croquettes back onto the cookie sheet lined with parchment paper. When all croquettes have been breaded, cover with plastic wrap or aluminum foil and refrigerate for 3 to 4 hours.

8. Fill a large skillet with oil, deep enough to cover an entire croquette and heat over medium-high heat to 350°F. (If you prefer, you can use a deep fryer to cook the croquettes.)

9. Using tongs, carefully place croquettes (in batches of about 6 to 8 croquettes at a time) into heated oil and fry for about 4 to 5 minutes, until deep brown on all sides, turning over once about halfway through. Remove from oil using tongs and transfer to plate lined with paper towels to absorb excess oil.

10. While cooking remaining batches, the fried croquettes may be kept warm in the oven heated to 175°F to 200°F for up to 30 minutes.

11. Serve with crackers and lime wedges.

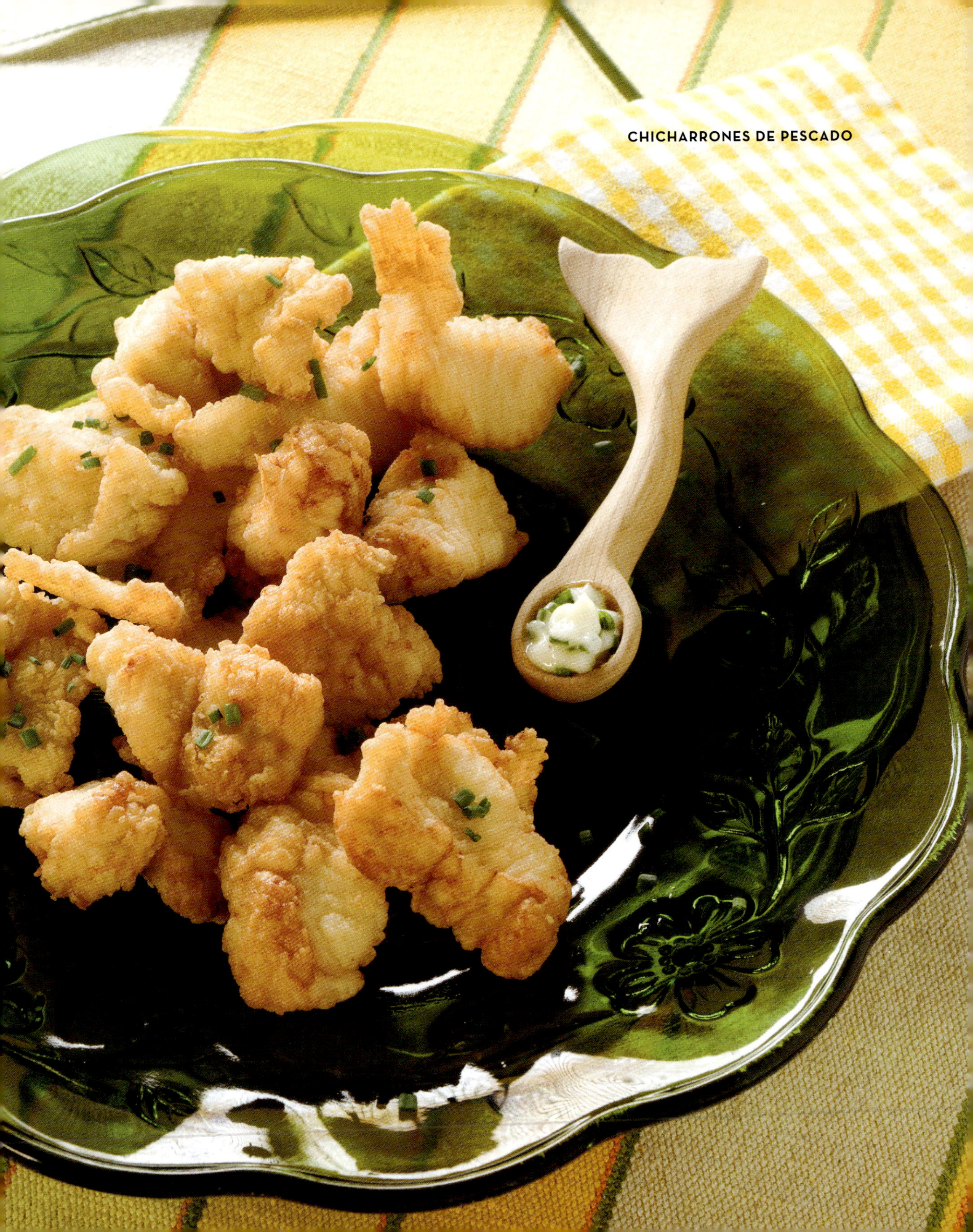
CHICHARRONES DE PESCADO

# Chicharrones de Pescado

(FRIED FISH CHUNKS)

---

*T*hese breaded fish chunks are one of my favorite appetizers.

The fish varies according to your taste. You can use snapper, sea bass, grouper, swordfish, pompano, or tuna. Corvina and mahimahi also work well. Just about any fish you like. Make sure that before you cut the fillets into chunks, you remove any bones that may have remained hidden in the fish fillet.

To give the fish more flavor, we let them soak in a marinade of spices, garlic, and lime juice before we bread them. That gives the fish a subtle touch of flavor that adds to the meat's natural taste.

Serve them with some lime wedges on the side for people who like to give them an extra splash of lime juice.

—*Emilio*

---

## YIELD: 6 TO 8 SERVINGS

pinch of cumin powder

1/4 tsp dried oregano

3/4 tsp salt

4 lbs fillet of grouper

3 cloves garlic, minced

juice from 2 limes

1 1/2 cups all-purpose flour

vegetable oil

2 or 3 sprigs of fresh parsley

2 limes cut into wedges for serving

1. In a small bowl, mix together the cumin, oregano, and salt.

2. Cut the fish fillets into chunks of approximately 1½" × 1½" and place them in a large bowl. Sprinkle the spice mixture evenly over the fish chunks. Then add

the garlic and lime juice. Let the fish chunks sit in the marinade for approximately 15 minutes.

3. Place the flour in a large bowl and dredge the marinated fish chunks in the flour.

4. Fill a large skillet just deep enough to cover the fish chunks about halfway and heat over medium-high heat to 360°F.

5. Fry the fish chunks in the heated oil for 6 to 8 minutes, turning over once about halfway through. Remove the fish from the skillet and transfer to a plate lined with paper towels to absorb excess oil.

6. Transfer the fish to a serving platter, garnish with parsley, and serve immediately with some lime wedges on the side.

# Frituras de Bacalao

(CODFISH FRITTERS)

———⊶⊷———

Frituras de bacalao *are like Cuban conch fritters, made with codfish instead of conch. The codfish we call* bacalao *is a coldwater fish that's been cured in salt.*

*Soaking the salted cod in water for a day or more allows it to regain its moisture and prepares it for cooking. If you are planning on making cod for tomorrow night's dinner, for example, start soaking it the afternoon before. Change the water a couple of times before bed and, depending on how salty you like it, a few more times before you cook it. The more you change the water, the less salty the cod will be when you eat it.*

—*Emilio*

———⊶⊷———

## YIELD: 12 TO 15 FRITTERS

2 cups (approximately 2 lbs) *bacalao* (salt-cured codfish)

1 cup self-rising flour

2 egg yolks, beaten

1 tsp salt

¼ tsp Bijol (optional for cooking)

4 tbsp minced onion

4 tbsp sliced scallion

4 tbsp *vino seco*

vegetable oil for frying

1. Rinse the *bacalao* under cool water for 5 to 10 minutes. Place the *bacalao* in a baking dish and cover it with water and soak it overnight in the refrigerator. Change the water once or twice if you want to further reduce the salt content. Drain and place the *bacalao* into a pan. Cover it with water and bring to a boil.

Reduce the heat, cover and cook until the *bacalao* has softened. Remove the *bacalao* from the pan, reserve 1 cup of the fish broth, and rinse the cooked *bacalao* under cool running water for at least 10 minutes.

2. Flake the *bacalao* into a bowl. In a large bowl, whisk the flour with the reserved cup of fish broth). Add the remaining ingredients, including the flaked *bacalao*, and mix thoroughly.

3. Fill a large skillet with vegetable oil about halfway and heat the oil over medium-high heat to 360°F.

4. Working in batches, scoop tablespoon-sized dollops of the fritter dough and carefully drop them in the pan. Fry each batch for approximately 4 to 5 minutes, turning over once about halfway through. Fritters will float to the top and have a golden brown color when they are done. Remove the fritters from the oil and transfer them to a plate lined with paper towels to absorb excess oil. Then serve immediately.

FRITURAS DE MALANGA

# Frituras de Malanga

(MALANGA FRITTERS)

⊶⊷

There are certain things that have very personal memories for me. Frituras de malanga *are one of those things. My mother loved to make them, and I loved to eat them.*

Frituras de malanga *are basically* malanga *fritters. They're similar to the* frituras de bacalao, *except that they replace the salted codfish with* malanga.

Malanga, *or taro root, is a leafy plant with a large edible root. In Cuba,* malanga *is served boiled, mashed, or fried. They're all tasty, but freshly made* frituras de malanga *are one of my favorite foods. I still remember watching my mother make them.*

—*Emilio*

⊶⊷

## YIELD: APPROXIMATELY 12 TO 15 FRITTERS

1 lb *malangas,* peeled and washed thoroughly

½ onion, peeled

1 tsp salt

1 clove garlic, minced

1 tsp chopped parsley

2 egg yolks

vegetable oil

1. Grate the *malangas* and the onion and place them in a large bowl.

2. Add the salt, garlic, parsley, and egg yolks. Combine thoroughly to form a *malanga* "batter."

3.  Fill a large skillet with vegetable oil about halfway and heat over medium-high heat to 360°F.

4.  Working in batches, scoop tablespoon-sized dollops of the fritter dough and carefully drop them into the pan. Fry each batch for approximately 4 to 5 minutes, until golden brown on all sides, turning over once about halfway through. Remove the fritters from the oil and transfer them to a plate lined with paper towels to absorb excess oil. Serve immediately.

ENSALADA DE AGUACATE

# Ensalada de Aguacate

(AVOCADO SALAD)

⟨⟨⟩⟩

As you might notice, there are not a lot of green salads or conventional vegetables in Cuban cuisine. The only vegetables are pretty much the plantain, yuca, and malanga, which we love.

But a simple and delicious salad that is a regular offering with a typical Cuban meal is ensalada de aguacate, or avocado salad. That's one salad that we love, love, love.

Some people like it with onion. I like it plain with oil, vinegar, and salt. That to me is my favorite because avocados have such a delicious taste. They're creamy and smooth in texture, with a subtle, unique flavor.

*—Gloria*

⟨⟨⟩⟩

## YIELD: 4 SERVINGS

3 oz olive oil

3 oz white vinegar

salt to taste

1 large avocado, in season

1/2 medium red onion, coarsely chopped

1. In a small bowl, whisk the olive oil, vinegar, and salt.

2. Peel and slice the avocado.

3. Place the avocado and onions in a salad bowl, and then toss gently.

4. Drizzle the dressing over the salad and serve immediately.

Soups

GLORIA COOKING WITH HER MOTHER, GLORIA FAJARDO

*I*N CUBAN TRADITION you have two things that everyone typically eats every day. One is *frijoles negros* (black beans). The other thing is soup.

In my house, my mother made a soup every night. Whether it was plantain or chicken soup, when I was a kid, my mother would always serve a soup before we ate dinner.

When you talk about something that's truly *comida criolla,* there's nothing more typical than a *malanga* soup or a plantain soup.

*Malanga* is a root vegetable similar to a yam in the way it looks. We'll eat *malangas* as a side dish, chop them up to flavor other dishes, or make a delicious thick and succulent soup: *crema de malanga.* Think of it as a cream of potato soup, Cuban style.

Plantains, or *plátanos,* as we call them, are a major part of just about every Cuban meal. We adopted them as a staple in our cuisine. We'll eat them in every stage of maturity from green to mushy ripe. We mash them, boil them, fry them, and—as we'll show you in a few pages—make them the chief ingredient in their very own soup. It's rich and creamy, and one of my favorites.

Lentil and split pea soups are also standards in a lot of Cuban kitchens, along with chicken soup. We don't just eat it when it's cold out or when sick with the flu. For us, *sopa de pollo* is a regular meal starter. Typically, Cuban chicken soup has noodles, potatoes, and carrots, and our standard mix of onions and garlic for flavor. We also like to squeeze some lime juice on the chicken soup, giving the soup some zest.

As I said, at a Cuban table, soup is a starter. But you may find that any of these soups are filling enough to be a meal by themselves.

—*Emilio*

SOPA DE POLLO

# Sopa de Pollo

## (CHICKEN SOUP)

───❀───

I n our culture, we serve most of the food together—the main course and the salad tend to come out at the same time, for example.

But we do serve soup before the rest of the meal as a regular part of a typical dinner. Soup serves as our appetizer.

One of my favorites is sopa de pollo. Even though the name is simply "chicken soup," it would probably be more accurate to call it "chicken noodle soup" in English, because it's made with angel-hair pasta or vermicelli.

We also use a touch of Bijol, which adds a golden hue and a distinct flavor to the soup. Bijol is the same condiment we use in arróz con pollo (chicken and rice) and paella. And like with most chicken soups in other cuisines, it also has potatoes, carrots, and onions.

—Gloria

───❀───

### YIELD: 6 TO 8 SERVINGS

1 whole chicken

12 cups water

3 potatoes, cut into bite-sized pieces

2 carrots, peeled and sliced crosswise in 1/2" pieces

1/2 onion, finely chopped

2 cloves garlic, minced

1/4 tsp dried oregano

1 or 2 saffron strands or 1/4 tsp Bijol (for coloring)

3 oz angel-hair pasta or vermicelli

1 tbsp salt

2 limes, cut into wedges for serving

1. Cut the chicken into pieces, separating the various parts. Place it in a large pot and add the water and all the other ingredients except the saffron, pasta, salt, and limes. Bring to a boil, and then reduce the heat to low. Cook for 1 to 1½ hours, until chicken is cooked and completely tender.

2. Remove the chicken from the pot and skin and debone it, breaking it into bite-sized pieces. Return the chicken to the simmering broth.

3. Add the saffron and pasta, and cook the pasta according to the directions on package.

4. Add salt (feel free to increase or decrease the amount of salt). Serve the soup hot with one or two lime quarters, which can be squeezed over the soup according to taste.

### Tip from the Kitchen

Bijol is a powder made from ground annatto seeds, frequently used as a coloring agent in place of saffron. It is available at most Latin supermarkets or in the Latin aisle of your local grocery store.

CREMA DE MALANGA

# Crema de Malanga

(CREAM OF MALANGA [TARO ROOT] SOUP)

⸎

When you talk about true comida criolla, *few things are more typically Cuban than a cream of* malanga *soup.*

Crema de malanga *is like a cream of potato soup, made with* malangas *instead of potatoes, and it's one of my favorites.*

*—Emilio*

⸎

**YIELD: 8 SERVINGS**

2 lbs *malangas*, peeled and diced

4 quarts chicken stock

1 tbsp salt

1 small onion, minced

3 cloves garlic, minced

½ tbsp olive oil for sautéing

1 tsp fresh culantro, chopped

1. Place the *malangas*, chicken stock, salt and half of the minced onion in a large stockpot and bring to a boil. Reduce heat to medium low and simmer for approximately 45 to 60 minutes or until the *malangas* are tender. Remove from heat and let cool. Purée the contents of the stockpot in a blender (working in batches as necessary) and return it to the stockpot.

2. In a small skillet, sauté the remaining onion and the garlic in the olive oil, until translucent.

3. Fold the onion-garlic *sofrito* and the culantro into the soup and stir well.

4. Reheat the soup to desired temperature, then serve.

SOPA DE PLÁTANO

# Sopa de Plátano

## (PLANTAIN SOUP)

---

Next to malanga *soup (crema de malanga), plantain soup is probably one of the most traditional Cuban dishes.*

*Plantains are one of the most versatile vegetables in Cuban cuisine. We eat them boiled, fried, and mashed, and it doesn't matter if they're green or completely ripe.*

*For sopa de plátano, we use green plantains, peeled and sliced crosswise the same way you would cut up a banana to go on cereal. They're boiled and then puréed the same as malangas are for* crema de malanga, *and considering the thick, creamy consistency of the finished product, this dish probably should be called* crema de plátano.

—Emilio

---

### YIELD: 6 TO 8 SERVINGS

4 quarts beef or vegetable stock

1 cube chicken bouillon

6 large green plantains, sliced cross-wise into medium-sized chunks

¼ tsp salt

1 bay leaf

4 garlic cloves, minced

1 large onion, sliced

1 tbsp coarsley chopped fresh culantro, for garnish

1. Place the chicken or vegetable stock in a large stockpot and bring it to a boil over high heat. Reduce heat to medium and add the remaining ingredients except the culantro.

2. Cover, reduce heat to low, and simmer for approximately 30 minutes, until the plantains are tender. Remove the bay leaf.

3. Transfer the mixture to a blender and puree. Transfer the pureed soup back into the stockpot and cook over low heat uncovered for 15 to 20 minutes to allow the soup to thicken. Serve in bowls and garnish with culantro tips.

# Potaje de Frijoles Colorados

(RED BEAN SOUP)

⚬⚬⚬

Potaje *literally means "stew."*

*It's sometimes eaten alone, and it's sometimes eaten over rice. You have that option. You can also use black beans in place of the red, if you prefer.*

*Whichever you use, the key to a good* potaje *is the sofrito. That sautéed blend of olive oil, garlic, onion, bell pepper, and tomato paste gives the beans a true* criollo *flavor.*

*Adding Spanish-style chorizo sausage (making it into something closer to a stew) gives the* potaje *extra flavor.*

—Emilio

⚬⚬⚬

## YIELD: 6 TO 8 SERVINGS

1 lb small red beans (also referred to as Mexican red beans)

2 liters water, plus more as desired

2 tbsp olive oil

1/2 large white onion, finely chopped

1/2 green or red bell pepper, cored, seeded, and finely chopped

2 cloves garlic, crushed (using a garlic press or mortar and pestle)

3 tbsp tomato paste

1/2 tsp salt

1/4 tsp freshly ground black pepper

1 Spanish-style chorizo, casing removed and chopped

2 Russet potatoes, peeled and quartered

1/4 calabaza or butternut squash, peeled and cut into chunks

1 green plantain, peeled and cut into chunks (optional)

POTAJE DE FRIJOLES COLORADOS

1.  Rinse the beans thoroughly and remove any debris. Place the rinsed beans in a large stockpot and add the water. Over medium-high heat, bring the beans to a boil. Then cover the pan and reduce the heat to medium. Allow the beans to cook until almost tender, approximately 45 minutes.

2.  Meanwhile, prepare a *sofrito* that will be added to the soup for flavoring. In a large skillet, heat the olive oil over medium heat until fragrant. Then add the onions and bell peppers and stir-fry for 3 to 4 minutes, until the onions are translucent. Add the garlic, tomato paste, salt, pepper, and chorizos, and cook for another 2 minutes.

3.  Once the beans are almost tender, add the *sofrito*, potatoes, and calabaza and, if desired, the plantains to the beans. Cook the *potaje* over low heat for approximately 45 to 60 minutes or until the beans, potatoes, and calabaza are fully cooked and fork tender, and the soup has reached your desired consistency. (Add additional water, as necessary, if you prefer a "soupier" version.)

### Tip from the Kitchen

Calabaza is a pumpkin used for cooking in many Caribbean cuisines. It is not the pumpkin you typically carve at Halloween, although it looks like a small, very round pumpkin. It closely resembles butternut squash in texture and flavor. Calabaza is available at Latin supermarkets. If you can't find any, you may use butternut squash instead.

SOPA DE CHÍCHAROS

# Sopa de Chícharos

## (SPLIT PEA SOUP)

———✹———

Split pea soup is a dish that every culture has a variation of. The sofrito gives it a unique flavor you won't find anywhere else.

Sofrito serves as the base for several traditional Cuban dishes, but the exact ingredients of the sofrito vary depending on which one. For a potaje de frijoles colorados we sauté the onions and garlic together. For split pea soup, we add in smoked ham. The result is a distinctly rich flavor unlike any other split pea soup.

—*Gloria*

———✹———

### YIELD: 6 SERVINGS

- 1 lb dried split peas
- 4 cups water
- 4 cups chicken stock
- 1 smoked ham hock
- ½ tsp salt
- 3 tbsp olive oil
- 1 medium onion, finely chopped
- 1 large green bell pepper, cored, seeded, and finely chopped
- 1 large potato, quartered and cut into bite-sized chunks
- 1 lb calabaza or butternut squash, peeled and cut into chunks
- pinch of cumin powder

1. Rinse the split peas thoroughly and remove any debris. Place the rinsed split peas in a large stockpot and add the water, chicken stock, ham hock, and salt. Over medium heat, bring the mixture to a boil. Then reduce the heat to low. Simmer on low heat for approximately one hour.

2. Meanwhile, prepare a *sofrito* that will be added to the soup for flavoring. In a large skillet, heat the olive oil over medium heat until fragrant. Then add the onions and bell peppers and stir-fry for 3 to 4 minutes, until the onions are translucent. Add the ham and sauté for another 3 to 4 minutes.

3. After the soup has simmered for an hour, remove the ham hock and tear meat from the bones. Coarsley chop the ham meat and place back into the stockpot. Add the *sofrito*, potatoes, calabaza, and cumin to the split peas. Cover (with the lid slightly ajar) and continue to simmer, stirring occasionally, for another 25 to 30 minutes or until the potatoes and calabaza are fully cooked and fork tender.

4. If you want a thicker soup, simmer uncovered for an additional 10 to 15 minutes, but keep an eye on the soup to avoid overcooking. If your soup is too thick, add additional water and chicken stock (in equal parts).

### Tip from the Kitchen

You can substitute the ham hock with a Spanish-style chorizo (casings removed). Or, for a vegetarian version, use vegetable stock and leave out ham.

SOPA DE LENTEJAS

# Sopa de Lentejas

### (LENTIL SOUP)

⸺∞⸺

The popularity of lentil soup in Cuba is a sign of the Arabic influence in our heritage. The Moors ruled portions of Spain for almost eight hundred years, right up to the year Columbus discovered the New World. It's no wonder they left a mark on the cuisine that was transported to Cuba by the Spanish settlers.

It's also not very surprising that the Moors would have brought their love of lentil soup to Spain. Lentil soup is such an old dish that it's actually mentioned in the Bible.

But, as with most dishes that made their way to the island, Cubans modified it and made it their very own. The secret to the flavor of Cuban-style lentil soup again is the sautéed sofrito and its blend of garlic, onions, and pepper.

If you're a fan of lentil soup, making it our way will give you a deliciously different version that I'm sure you will love (as I do).

—Gloria

⸺∞⸺

## YIELD: 6 SERVINGS

1 lb dried lentils

4 cups water

4 cups chicken or vegetable stock

1/2 tsp salt

3 tbsp olive oil

1 medium onion, finely chopped

1 large green bell pepper, cored, seeded, and finely chopped

1/2 lb smoked ham steak, diced (optional)

1 large potato, quartered and cut into bite-sized pieces

1 lb calabaza or butternut squash, peeled and cut into chunks

pinch of cumin powder

1. Rinse lentils thoroughly and remove any debris. Place the rinsed lentils in a large stockpot, and add the water, chicken stock, and salt. Over medium heat, bring to a boil. Then reduce the heat to low. Simmer on low heat for approximately one hour.

2. Meanwhile, prepare a *sofrito* that will be added to the soup for flavoring. In a large skillet, heat the olive oil over medium heat until fragrant. Then add the onions and bell peppers and stir-fry for 3 to 4 minutes, until the onions are translucent. Add the ham and sauté for another 3 to 4 minutes.

3. Add the *sofrito*, potatoes, calabaza, and cumin to the lentils. Cover (with the lid slightly ajar) and simmer, stirring occasionally, for another 25 to 30 minutes, or until potatoes and calabaza are fully cooked and fork tender.

4. If you want a thicker soup, simmer uncovered for an additional 10 to 15 minutes, but keep an eye on the soup to avoid overcooking. If your soup is too thick, add additional water and chicken stock (in equal parts).

**Tip from the Kitchen**

For a vegetarian version, use vegetable stock and leave out ham.

Entrées

EMILIO HAVING DINNER

M OST CUBANS HAVE an ongoing love affair with meat. Whether it's beef, pork, or chicken, we love it!

The seasoning is simple; the result is delicious. Generally, we rely on the usual suspects: garlic, lime or bitter orange, and onions. Sometimes, we add tomato paste for a rich, succulent, and flavorful *sofrito*.

Some of our meat dishes have interesting names like "old clothes" (*ropa vieja*) and "fried cow" (*vaca frita*).

*Ropa vieja* tastes nothing like its name. It's a flank steak shredded into strips, blended with green peppers, tomatoes, onions, and garlic, and cooked slowly until it comes out looking like the tattered remnants of old clothing—hence the name.

All the recipes are born of native ingredients and islander ingenuity, mixed with the meats and culinary customs the early Spanish settlers brought with them.

Over time, other influences mixed in as well—African, French, English, and, later, Chinese. They combined with the "waste not, want not" mentality of the pioneers. *Ropa vieja* actually comes from reusing the meat used to make broth. After the flank steak is boiled, the meat is shredded and sautéed along with the *sofrito*; then it is cooked slowly to soak up the flavors.

*Vaca frita* is basically the same flank steak, boiled with garlic, onion, and salt, then pounded, marinated, and seared with onions. It has a tangier taste that's not as sweet as *ropa vieja*, but just as delicious.

Those are regular offerings at just about any Cuban table, as is *picadillo*. When I was a boy, my mother made *boliche*, the Cuban pot roast, regularly on Saturday nights and *palomilla* steaks at least once a week. She served the steaks topped with steaming onions and a squeeze of lime juice. *Arróz con pollo*, chicken and rice, was the Sunday dish, and I can still see my family gathered around the large table.

*Lechón asado* is usually served on holidays and special occasions. For Cubans, roast pork means Christmas the same way turkey says Thanksgiving in the United States.

And while meats may have been the basis for most of our favorite *comida criolla*, seafood naturally played an important part in the island's cuisine. The shrimp creole, *camarones enchilados*, is one of my personal favorites, and brings back great memories every time I smell it cooking.

The selection of dishes here presents truly typical Cuban foods. They are part of my culture, of my traditions, of my childhood, and of my life. Through them, you will know more about who we are, about my family, and our traditions.

These are our flavors. These are our foods. Enjoy!

—*Emilio*

BISTEC DE PALOMILLA

# Bistec de Palomilla

(CUBAN-STYLE STEAK)

P alomilla *is the most Cuban of steaks. And it's another one of those dishes that I can still smell—the garlic, lime, and onions all cooking together—just thinking about it.*

*It's basically a sirloin steak or a round steak, but rather than leaving it thick, Cuban style calls for it to be pounded or pressed until it's just ¼" to ⅜" thick.*

*You can use a meat mallet to flatten the steak. (I recommend you put it between two pieces of wax paper, to keep the juices from splattering all over the place.) Or you can ask your butcher to press it for you. Either way, you want the steak to be as evenly thin as possible. Instead of just cooking the meat and adding garlic and limes, it's important to let it marinate so that the meat absorbs the flavor before you cook it.*

*Because the meat is so thin, this dish is also quick to make. It only takes a couple of minutes per side for the steaks to be cooked. Then you reduce what's left of the marinade in the cooking juices for a minute or two before you pour it back over the steaks on the plate.*

*You can also bread the steak, if you like, although I like the traditional style.*

—Emilio

**GARNISH:**

1 cup parsley, coarsely chopped

½ medium onion, finely chopped

 olive oil

6 8-oz boneless steaks (sirloin preferred, but you can use top round)

juice of 1 lime, or from 1 *naranja agria* (sour orange)

3 cloves garlic, minced

1½ tsp salt

1 tsp freshly ground black pepper

olive oil

2 limes, cut into wedges for serving

1. Prepare the garnish. In a medium bowl, combine the parsley and chopped onion, and drizzle a small amount of olive oil over the mixture. Do not add too much olive oil or the topping will get soggy. Cover with plastic wrap and set aside.

2. Place the steaks between sheets of wax paper. Then pound the steaks using a meat mallet until each steak is between ¼" and ⅜" thick.

> ### Tip from the Kitchen
>
> The chefs at our restaurants use a meat press to obtain an even thickness. You might ask your butcher to press the meat for you.

3. In a small bowl, combine the lime juice or *naranja agria* (you can substitute the *naranja agria* juice with 2 parts lemon juice to 1 part orange juice in any recipe in this cookbook), garlic, salt, and pepper. Place the steaks in a sealable plastic bag and add the garlic-lime marinade. Let the steaks marinate in the refrigerator for about an hour, turning the bag once or twice to ensure all steaks are evenly covered. Remove the steaks from the marinade and pat dry with paper towels, making sure no bits of garlic remain on the meat. Reserve the marinade.

4. In a large skillet, heat about 1 tablespoon of olive oil over high heat. (If the olive oil starts to smoke, you've overheated it and should discard it and start

with fresh olive oil.) Place 1 or 2 steaks into the skillet at a time and cook for 1 to 2 minutes per side. Then remove the steaks and set them aside. (Add olive oil between batches, as necessary.)

5.  Once all the steaks are cooked, add the reserved marinade and bring to a boil over medium-high heat, and reduce the juices for approximately 1 to 2 minutes. Pour the juices on top of the steaks and top with the garnish.

6.  Serve the steaks with lime wedges so that additional lime juice may be squeezed over each steak, to taste.

## Tip from the Kitchen

Palomilla steak is traditionally served with white rice, black beans, and *plátanos maduros*, or you can substitute the white rice and black beans with *moros*. Some folks prefer their *palomilla* served with shoestring French fries—the Cuban version of the French *steak frites*.

VACA FRITA

# Vaca Frita

—∞—

I only ate vaca frita *after I left Cuba, so for me it represents Miami more than Cuba. I was more accustomed to eating* ropa vieja *in Cuba.*

*Both are testaments to the Cuban cook's thriftiness.*

Vaca frita *literally means "fried cow," a rather simple way of describing the dish's basic ingredient. In fact, though, the meat is boiled before it's fried. That's because, like* ropa vieja, vaca frita *is made with skirt steak or flank steak that's been boiled to make broth. Rather than waste a good piece of meat, frugal Cuban cooks found ways to turn it into a delicious main course.*

*At least that's the way it used to be. Now the meat is cooked specifically to make either* vaca frita *or* ropa vieja, *and nobody worries about the broth.*

*In both cases, the boiled steak ends up with a shredded appearance. The main difference is that* vaca frita *is sautéed quickly with onions and* ropa vieja *is wetter, cooked with tomatoes and peppers.*

—Emilio

—∞—

3 lbs flank steak

8 cups water, plus additional water as needed

1¹/₂ tsp salt

8 cloves garlic, minced

1 medium onion, chopped

1 tsp dried oregano

1 bay leaf

¹/₂ cup lime juice

vegetable oil for searing

olive oil for sautéing

1 medium white onion, thinly sliced into rings

2 limes, cut into wedges for serving

1. Place the meat into a large pot and cover with the water. Add 1 teaspoon of salt, about half of the minced garlic, and the chopped onion.

2. Bring the mixture to a boil over medium-high heat. Then reduce to medium-low heat, and cook uncovered for 60 to 90 minutes until the meat is tender, adding additional water as needed to make sure the meat doesn't dry out.

3. Remove meat from pot and allow to cool. Cut the meat as necessary to yield 6 steaks. Using the spiked end of a meat mallet, carefully pound the cooked meat to about ½" thickness. The flattened meat should have a shredded appearance. Transfer the pounded steaks into a large baking dish, then add the remaining garlic, oregano, bay leaf, lime juice, and ½ teaspoon of salt, spreading evenly over the steaks. Refrigerate and marinate the meat for 2 to 3 hours. When you're ready to cook, remove the steaks from marinade and pat dry with paper towels, making sure no bits of garlic remain.

4. Lightly grease a large skillet with vegetable oil and heat over high heat. (Be careful not to overheat the oil, but the pan needs to be hot enough to allow you to sear the meat.) Working in batches, take 1 or 2 of the steaks at a time and sear about 1 to 2 minutes per side until the meat is browned and has a crispy texture on the outside. Remove and set aside. (Using a paper towel, carefully regrease the skillet between batches as necessary.)

5. Once all steaks are seared and set aside, wipe the skillet with a paper towel, add 1 tablespoon of olive oil to the pan and heat over medium-high heat.

Sauté the onions in the pan for about 4 to 5 minutes or until the onions are translucent.

6.  Pour the sautéed onions over the steaks and serve the steaks with lime wedges.

CARNE CON PAPAS

# Carne con Papas

(BEEF STEW WITH POTATOES)

⁜

Carne con papas *is beef stew for Cubans.*

*It's one of my favorites because I love all tomato-based things and* carne con papas *has a very flavorful tomato sauce base. It's great just to soak up the sauce with a piece of bread once you're done eating the meat and vegetables. But, actually, my favorite thing is to mix the sauce with white rice. Sometimes I would ask my grandma just for the sauce and the rice.*

*What's great, too, is that because the potatoes cook in the sauce, they absorb that flavor, which gives them a sweetness that's delicious.*

*The most important thing with* carne con papas *is the cut of meat you use to make it. To make really good* carne con papas, *you have to use chuck, bottom round or short-rib meat (my personal favorite meat to use is veal chunks). Do that, and use a good, dry cooking wine, and you'll have people begging you to make it, again and again.*

—Gloria

⁜

½ cup olive oil

3 lbs boneless stewing beef (chuck, bottom round, or short-rib meat), cut into 2" x 2" cubes

1 tbsp salt

½ tsp freshly ground black pepper

1 tsp paprika

pinch of cumin powder

1 large onion, chopped

3 cloves garlic, crushed (using a garlic press or mortar and pestle)

1 green pepper, cored, seeded, and finely chopped

2 bay leaves

1 8-oz can tomato sauce

½ cup *vino seco* or dry white wine, and more as necessary

4 cups water, and more as necessary

½ cup pimento-stuffed Spanish olives

3 large potatoes, peeled and cut into medium-sized chunks

2 carrots, sliced crosswise into medium-sized chunks

1. In a large pot, heat the olive oil. Then sauté the meat over medium-high heat for 3 to 4 minutes, turning frequently, until lightly browned.

2. Add the salt, pepper, paprika, cumin, onion, garlic, green pepper, and bay leaves, and stir-fry until the onions are translucent. Add the tomato sauce, *vino seco*, and water. Bring the mixture to a boil. Then reduce heat, cover, and simmer over low heat until meat is tender, about 1½ hours.

3. Add the stuffed olives, potatoes, and carrots. Then cover and cook for an additional 30 to 40 minutes, until the potatoes and carrots are tender. Check frequently and add additional water and *vino seco*, as necessary. Remove and discard bay leaves prior to serving.

PICADILLO

# Picadillo

(MINCED GROUND BEEF CREOLE)

———⚬⚬⚬———

Picadillo *is probably one of the most popular Cuban dishes.*

*Variations are found across Latin America and one of the key differences between Cuban-style* picadillo *and the way it's made in other countries is that we use pimento-stuffed Spanish olives in ours.*

*We like to use capers and raisins in our version, but you can omit them if you don't like them. The tomato sauce adds sweetness and makes the finished dish soupier than the way it's made in other places, and we usually serve it over white rice, with a helping of* maduros *and some black beans on the side.*

*A variation that my mother used to make at home in Cuba is called* a caballo, *or "on horseback." It just means she fried up some eggs and set one on top of each serving of* picadillo. *It is an option that makes the dish totally different and even more delicious!*

—*Emilio*

———⚬⚬⚬———

4 tsp olive oil

3 lbs lean ground beef

1 green pepper, cored, seeded, and finely chopped

1 medium onion, finely chopped

3 cloves garlic, minced

2 tsp salt

1/2 tsp ground black pepper

pinch of cumin powder

1 tsp dried oregano

2 bay leaves

1 8-oz can tomato sauce

1¼ cups *vino seco* or dry white wine

1/2 cup ketchup

1/2 cup raisins (optional)

1/2 cup pimento-stuffed Spanish olives

2 tbsp capers (optional)

PICADILLO A CABALLO

# A Caballo

**6 large eggs**

1. In a large pot, heat 1 teaspoon of olive oil over medium-high heat. Add the ground beef, and brown the meat, stirring occasionally and ensuring that the meat is not scorched. Remove the browned meat and drain any excess fat from the pot.

2. Add the remaining olive oil, and heat it over medium heat. Then add the green pepper, onion, and garlic, and sauté until the onions are translucent.

3. Return the browned meat to the pot, and add the remaining ingredients. Bring the mixture to a boil. Then reduce the heat to low, cover, and simmer the *picadillo* for 30 to 40 minutes, stirring frequently.

4. Remove the bay leaves and serve over white rice (see recipe on page 147) with *plátanos maduros* (*tostones,* if you prefer) and black beans.

> ## Tip from the Kitchen
>
> To make *picadillo a caballo* or "picadillo on horseback," just before serving, fry one egg per portion (over easy or over medium) and slide them onto the *picadillo.*

ROPA VIEJA

# Ropa Vieja

## (TORN BEEF)

━━━∞━━━

Ropa vieja *is something I've eaten all my life, but one of the memories that stands out for me every time I eat it is watching Gloria's grandmother make flank steak soup for us—how she grated the carrots and malanga and put them into the pot with the steak and boiling it to make the beef soup. Then, after the soup was done, she made* ropa vieja *with the boiled meat, and I can still smell the tomatoes, onions, and garlic as she sautéed them to make the* sofrito.

*That's the same way they made it in Cuba. It was a way to use the meat that was left over from making the soup, so it wouldn't go to waste.*

*It's said that settlers from the Canary Islands, off the coast of Spain, brought* ropa vieja *to Cuba. Luckily, it tastes nothing like its name. Ropa vieja means "old clothes," but it's called that only because when it's done cooking the blend of shredded meat, tomatoes, and green peppers looks like the tattered strips of a colorful dress.*

*—Emilio*

━━━∞━━━

3 lbs flank steak

12 cups water

2 tbsp olive oil

2 onions, sliced

4 cloves garlic, crushed (using a garlic press or mortar and pestle)

2 medium tomatoes, quartered and cut into wedges about 1/2" thick

3 green bell peppers, cored, seeded, and sliced

1 tsp Bijol

pinch of cumin powder

3 bay leaves

2 1/2 cups tomato sauce

1 cup *vino seco* or dry white wine

1. Place flank steak, water and salt in a deep pot or sauté pan, and bring it to a boil over medium-high heat. Reduce the heat to medium-low, and cook the beef for about an hour, until it starts to shred. Using a slotted spoon, remove the beef and set it aside to let cool. Reserve the water used to cook the beef.

2. Once the beef has sufficiently cooled, shred it as necessary (using your hands or a meat mallet) so it is broken up into strands and has a stringy appearance.

3. In a large covered pot or Dutch oven, heat the olive oil over medium heat until fragrant. Add the onions and cook for 2 minutes. Reduce heat to medium, and add the garlic, tomatoes, green peppers, salt, Bijol, cumin, bay leaves, tomato sauce, and the shredded beef. Cook for 4 to 5 minutes, stirring occasionally.

4. Add the reserved water and *vino seco*, bring the mixture to a gentle boil, and then reduce the heat to low, cover, and simmer for an additional 20 minutes.

5. Remove the bay leaves and serve hot over white rice (see recipe on page 147).

BOLICHE

# Boliche

(CUBAN POT ROAST)

⸻

When I was growing up, my mother had a weekly menu, of sorts. Every Sunday, she made arróz con pollo (chicken and rice). On Saturdays, we ate boliche. And, boy, did I look forward to Saturdays.

Boliche is a Cuban pot roast, seasoned with naranja agria, oregano, and garlic, then cooked slowly with white wine, chicken broth, and onions, until the meat is so tender it practically melts in your mouth. That's the way we cook most meats in Cuba, slowly, so that they're falling off the bone by the time that we serve them. But cooking the boliche slowly allows the meat to soak up the garlic and wine.

Like with ropa vieja and carne con papas, some people like to just serve the boliche over white rice so that the sauce and rice mix. Or you might want to have some Cuban bread on hand so you can soak up the sauce with it while you eat the meat.

—Emilio

⸻

## YIELD: 6 TO 8 SERVINGS

8 cloves garlic, crushed (using a garlic press or mortar and pestle)

1 cup *naranja agria* (sour orange) juice

1 tsp dried oregano

5-lb eye round

1 cup vegetable oil

3 large white onions, sliced

1 cup *vino seco* or dry white wine

3 bay leaves

2 1/2 cups chicken broth

1. Make the marinade by combining the garlic, *naranja agria* (you can substitute the *naranja agria* juice with 2 parts lemon juice to 1 part orange juice in any recipe in this cookbook), and oregano in a mixing bowl. Pierce the eye round with a fork, then place in a deep bowl, add marinade and refrigerate overnight.

2. When you are ready to cook, remove the meat from baking dish and reserve the marinade. In a large pot or Dutch oven, heat the vegetable oil over medium-high heat so it is hot enough to sear the meat. Then add the roast and brown on all sides, being careful not to scorch it.

3. Remove the meat and set aside. Add the onions and sauté for 2 to 3 minutes. Reduce heat to medium, add the reserved marinade and allow to simmer for approximately 5 minutes. Add the *vino seco*, bay leaves, chicken broth and meat. Then reduce the heat to medium low and cover the pot, leaving the lid slightly ajar.

4. Simmer the ingredients for approximately 75 minutes. Remove the meat from the pot and slice against the grain into ½-inch thick slices, then place the sliced meat back into the pot and simmer over low heat for another 60 to 90 minutes or until meat is tender.

5. When meat is suffciently tender, remove it from the pot and reserve the cooking juices. Working in batches, take about 1 cup of the cooked onions and pan juices at a time and pass through a sieve into a bowl to make a serving sauce.

6. Top off each serving of *boliche* slices with some of the serving sauce and serve with white rice and black beans and plantains or *plátanos maduros* on the side.

### Tip from the Kitchen

Gloria's grandma, Consuelo, used to make a variation of this dish known as *carne mechada*. To make *carne mechada*, prior to browning the meat, using a long knife, cut two slits lengthwise through the center of the eye round in the shape of an "x" and stuff a long Spanish-style chorizo (or two or three smaller ones) into the cavity. (Loosely translated into English, *carne mechada* means "meat with a wick," and the name was likely derived from the appearance of the chorizo inside the meat, which sort of looks like a wick embedded in a candle. Regardless of the origin of the term, the taste of the chorizo will penetrate the meat, giving it even more flavor than the "wickless" version.)

LECHÓN ASADO

# Lechón Asado

(CUBAN-STYLE ROASTED PORK)

For most Cubans, lechón asado is *always served for special occasions. More than anything, it's the main course in our* Noche Buena *(Christmas Eve) feasts, but we also serve it at weddings, baptisms, and just about any other special gathering. Usually, it involves roasting a whole pig, and making it becomes a celebration in itself.*

*The most important thing for my grandma was that the skin ended up really crispy. First she would cook the meat in sort of a steamlike atmosphere—either in a* caja china *or, if she was making a leg in the oven, wrapped in aluminum foil. That way, it would cook thoroughly, but remained moist. You don't want to roast pork without covering it because it will dry out.*

*Then, at the end, she would remove the foil to allow the skin to brown. That way, the fat had been cooked away, and the skin would end up so crispy, it was like a cracker. But the meat was juicy and tender and cooked completely through.*

*That's why for me the* caja china *is so great for cooking a whole pig. The* caja china *is an enclosed kind of barbecue that keeps the meat from drying out while it cooks. The name literally means "Chinese box," and although its exact origins are cloudy, it's pretty certain it was invented in Cuba specifically as a way to cook a whole pork. Nowadays, you can buy them over the Internet, and they're great for roasting pork.*

—Gloria

6 to 8 cups modified *mojo*\* (see recipe on page 159)

2 medium onions, minced

1 tsp cumin powder

1 cup *vino seco* or dry white wine

8- to 10-lb *pierna de puerco* (bone-in fresh ham, skin on)

olive oil

1 large onion, sliced

\* To modify the mojo for this dish, do not include the olive oil, as the pork has enough fat in it already.

1. Combine the *mojo,* minced onions, cumin, and *vino seco* in a medium bowl. The resulting marinade should have the consistency of a chunky sauce.

2. Rinse the pork under cold water and pat dry. Using a sharp knife, pierce the pork throughout. Place the pork in a deep roasting pan and pour the *mojo* over the pork; also rub the *mojo* all over the pork. (If you have a basting syringe, you may use it to inject the *mojo* into the pork.) Cover and refrigerate, and allow the pork to marinate for at least 24 hours, turning at least once.

3. Preheat oven to 325°F. Cover the pork with aluminum foil and cook for 4 to 5 hours—approximately 30 minutes per pound. Remove the foil during the last hour of roasting to allow the skin to brown. The *lechón* is done when the pork's internal temperature (using an instant-read thermometer) reaches 180°F.

4. Remove the roasted pork from the oven and transfer it to a cutting board and cover with aluminum foil. Transfer the pan juices to a fat separator and, once fat is removed, place the remaining juices in a gravy boat to pass around the table. (If you don't have a fat separator, pour the pan juices into a deep bowl and let cool. The fat will rise to the top and can be scooped out of the bowl.)

5. Carve the pork after it has rested for at least 15 minutes.

6. Heat 2 to 3 tablespoons of olive oil over medium heat until just fragrant, then add onions and sauté until the onions are translucent.

7. Top off each serving of *lechón* with some sautéed onions. Serve with white rice and black beans (or *moros,* if you prefer) and green or ripe fried plantains.

# Vaca Frita de Pollo

### (CUBAN-MOJO-MARINATED SHREDDED CHICKEN)

⎯⎯⎯ ◦∞∞◦ ⎯⎯⎯

I f it's chicken, it can't really be vaca frita, *but the name of this dish refers to the style of cooking and seasoning.*

Vaca frita *is usually made with a skirt steak or flank steak that's been boiled, then shredded, seasoned, and fried. It's nice and garlicky and great with lime juice squeezed over the top of it as it's steaming on your plate.*

*This version is made with chicken instead of steak, but is otherwise prepared the same way its beef namesake is made. The result is a lighter variation of the original that's perfect for chicken lovers.*

*—Emilio*

⎯⎯⎯ ◦∞∞◦ ⎯⎯⎯

## YIELD: 6 SERVINGS

6 large boneless, skinless chicken breasts

1¹⁄₂ tsp of salt

8 cloves garlic, minced

1 medium onion, chopped

1 tsp dried oregano

1 bay leaf

¹⁄₂ cup lime juice

8 cups water, plus additional water as needed

vegetable oil for searing

olive oil for sautéing

1 medium white onion, thinly sliced into rings

2 limes, cut into wedges for serving

1. Place the chicken into a large pot and cover with the water. Add 1 teaspoon of salt, about half of the minced garlic, and the chopped onion.

VACA FRITA DE POLLO

2. Bring the mixture to a boil over medium-high heat. Then reduce the heat to medium, and cook uncovered for 30 to 40 minutes until the chicken is fully cooked, adding additional water as needed to make sure the chicken doesn't dry out.

3. Remove the chicken from the pot and allow it to cool. Using the spiked end of a meat mallet, carefully pound each breast to flatten about ½-inch thickness. The flattened chicken breasts should have a somewhat-shredded appearance. Transfer the breasts to a large baking dish and add the remaining garlic, oregano, bay leaf, lime juice, and the remaining ½ teaspoon of salt, spreading evenly over the breasts. Refrigerate and marinate the chicken for 2 to 3 hours. When you're ready to cook, remove breasts from the marinade and pat dry with paper towels, making sure no bits of garlic remain.

4. Lightly grease a large skillet with vegetable oil and heat over high heat. (The pan needs to be hot enough to allow you to sear the meat but be careful not to overheat the oil.) Working in batches, take 1 or 2 of the breasts at a time and sear about 1 to 2 minutes per side until the meat is browned and has a crispy texture on the outside. Remove and set aside. (Using a paper towel, carefully regrease the skillet between batches as necessary.)

5. Once all the breasts have been seared and set aside, wipe the skillet with a paper towel, add 1 tablespoon of olive oil to the pan and heat over medium-high heat. Sauté the onions in the pan for about 4 to 5 minutes or until the onions are translucent.

6. Pour the sautéed onions over the chicken breasts and serve with the lime wedges.

ARRÓZ CON POLLO

# Arróz con Pollo

(CHICKEN AND YELLOW RICE)

※

When I was a kid growing up in Cuba, my entire family came over for dinner on Sundays. We gathered around the large kitchen table at my parents' house in Santiago, Cuba, and my mother would serve the most delicious arróz con pollo in the world.

Cuban-style chicken and rice gets its color from a touch of Bijol powder, which we sometimes use in place of saffron. It doesn't give the exact same flavor as saffron, but that's okay. It does give it its own uniquely Cuban flavor, and makes our arróz con pollo distinctive.

My mother made the rice "wet," not dry—what we call asopado or a la chorrera. But you can experiment with different amounts of chicken stock, water, and vino seco until you get yours exactly as dry or as wet as you like.

—Emilio

※

1 small jar *pimientos morrones* (roasted red peppers)

1/3 cup olive oil

2 whole chickens, bone in, skin on, quartered and cut into pieces

1 large white onion, chopped

1 green pepper, cored, seeded, and chopped

4 cloves garlic, crushed (using a garlic press or mortar and pestle)

2 tsp salt

1/2 tsp freshly ground black pepper

1 tsp Bijol powder

2 tsp dried oregano

pinch of cumin powder

1 bay leaf

1 cup tomato sauce

4 cups parboiled rice, thoroughly rinsed

1 quart chicken stock

4 cups water

1 cup *vino seco* or dry white wine

1/2 cup canned or frozen peas

1. Finely chop the *pimientos morrones* and reserve the liquid.

2. In a large pot or Dutch oven, heat the olive oil over medium-high heat until fragrant. Then lightly brown the chicken pieces. Remove the chicken and set aside.

3. Add the onions, green peppers, and garlic, and stir-fry the *sofrito* until the onions are translucent, about 3 to 4 minutes.

4. Add the chopped *pimientos morrones* and the reserved liquid, salt, pepper, Bijol, dried oregano, cumin powder, bay leaf, tomato sauce, and parboiled rice, and cook for 3 to 4 minutes, stirring frequently.

5. Add the chicken stock, water, *vino seco,* and browned chicken, and bring to a boil. Then reduce the heat to low, and cover and simmer for 30 to 40 minutes or until the chicken and the rice are fully cooked. Add the peas and cook for an additional 5 to 10 minutes. Remove the bay leaf before serving.

### Tip from the Kitchen

This version of *arróz con pollo* results in a drier rice. If you prefer a "soupier" rice, what we call *"asopado"* or *"a la chorrera,"* substitute the parboiled rice with short-grained (*Valencia*) rice and use 12 cups of water (instead of 4). You may need to cook it a bit longer than specified (before adding the peas) to get the rice to the desired "soupiness."

FRICASÉ DE POLLO

# Fricasé de Pollo

## (CHICKEN FRICASSEE)

———∞∞∞———

F ricasé de pollo *is similar to* carne con papas, *but made with chicken. It's basically chicken stew.*

*The sauce is what really makes the dish, and when you mix it with white rice, it's one of my favorite meals.*

*Chicken is a lot lighter than beef, and if you really want to make a dietetic dish, then cook the chicken without the skin. Since it's not cooked in the oven, you can remove the skin with less consequence because the sauce keeps the chicken very moist.*

*This is definitely one of those dishes that you want to enjoy with a piece of Cuban bread. Allowing the bread to soak up the sauce is heavenly!*

—Gloria

———∞∞∞———

2 whole chickens, bone in, skin on, quartered and cut into pieces

1 large onion, finely chopped

1 green bell pepper, cored, seeded, and finely chopped

1 red bell pepper, cored, seeded, and finely chopped

1 cup *vino* seco or dry white wine

1 8-oz tomato sauce

1/4 tsp salt

2 tsp dried oregano

pinch of cumin

1 tsp Bijol

3 cloves garlic, crushed (using a garlic press or mortar and pestle)

2 quarts chicken stock

2 carrots, peeled and sliced crosswise in 1/2" pieces

3 russet potatoes, peeled and quartered

1/2 cup pimento-stuffed olives (optional)

1. Place all the ingredients except the carrots and potatoes into a large covered pot or Dutch oven. Bring the mixture to a boil over medium-high heat. Then reduce the heat to medium, and cook for 45 minutes, stirring occasionally.

2. Add the carrots, potatoes, and stuffed olives, and cook for an additional 30 minutes or until the carrots and potatoes are fork tender.

3. Serve over white rice.

# Pollo Asado

## (ROASTED CHICKEN)

———∞———

Pollo asado, *otherwise known as "roasted chicken," is one of my all-time favorites. Roasted chicken is another dish that Cubans share with other world cuisines, but we make it our own with a salsa criolla used when roasting the chicken. And the lime juice gives it an extra kick. It is the exact recipe that my grandma used to make. The chicken is moist, while the skin remains crispy and very flavorful. I love it!*

—Gloria

———∞———

## YIELD: 4 SERVINGS

2 whole chickens

salt

dried oregano

3 cups *naranja agria* (sour orange) juice

6 cloves garlic, minced

**SALSA CRIOLLA:**

1/2 cup vegetable oil

1 medium onion, peeled and diced

1 green and 1 red bell pepper, cored, seeded and diced

2 cups tomato sauce

1 cup ketchup

4 cups water

2 tbsp garlic powder

1/2 tsp salt (or more to taste)

1 tbsp oregano

pinch of cumin powder

2 bay leaves

1 cup *vino seco*

olive oil for drizzling

POLLO ASADO

1. Remove the neck and giblets from the chicken, rinse thoroughly under cool tap water, and then pat dry, and cut each chicken in half. Sprinkle the chicken all over with the salt (generously) and oregano (lightly).

2. In a mixing bowl, combine the *naranja agria* juice (you can substitute the *naranja agria* juice with 2 parts lemon juice to 1 part orange juice in any recipe in this cookbook) with the garlic. Place the chicken skin side down in a baking dish, pour the *naranja agria*–garlic marinade all over it. Cover the chicken and refrigerate overnight.

3. About an hour before roasting the chicken, prepare a *salsa criolla* as follows: In a large saucepan or casserole, heat the vegetable oil over medium heat. Add the onion, then the peppers and sauté until the onions are translucent, about 3 to 4 minutes, then add the remaining ingredients except the *vino seco* and olive oil. Bring the sauce to a boil, then reduce the heat to low and simmer gently for about 30 minutes. Remove from heat and allow sauce to cool.

4. Position a rack in the center of the oven, and preheat the oven to 350°F. Remove the bay leaves. Pour the *salsa criolla* over the chicken halves, followed by the *vino seco* and a drizzling of olive oil. Flip the chicken halves over so they are skin side up, then cover the chicken with aluminum foil. Place the chicken in the oven and roast for 45 minutes. Then remove the foil and continue roasting for another 30 to 45 minutes to allow the skin to brown.

5. The chicken is done when an instant-read thermometer inserted into the thickest part of the thigh registers 170°F to 175°F.

6. Remove the chicken to a platter, and let it stand for 10 to 15 minutes, then serve.

PESCADO A LA PLANCHA

# *Pescado a la Plancha*

## (SAUTÉED FISH WITH GARLIC AND CITRUS)

———※———

S autéed fish can be really healthy, particularly if you use olive oil instead of butter to cook it. We marinate our fish with naranja agria and garlic before cooking it.

Emilio likes his fish very well done, so it's really dried and crispy. I like it when it's just cooked through, so it's not raw, but it's still juicy on the inside.

Sole always works great, because it's thin, but you can use just about any fish, depending on your taste. My favorites are grouper, snapper, sea bass, and mahimahi—fish that are native to the waters surrounding Florida and Cuba. They are delicious.

*—Gloria*

———※———

### YIELD: 8 SERVINGS

1½ cup *naranja agria* (sour orange) juice

1 tsp salt

pinch of black pepper

pinch of cumin powder

½ tsp dried oregano

4 cloves garlic, crushed (using a garlic press or mortar and pestle)

8 fillets of grouper (approximately 8 oz each)

olive oil

1. In a small mixing bowl, whisk the *naranja agria* juice (you can substitute the *naranja agria* juice with 2 parts lemon juice to 1 part orange juice in any recipe in this cookbook), salt, oregano, and crushed garlic.

2. Place the fillets in a deep baking dish, and pour the marinade over the fish, making sure each fillet is coated. Cover the fish with plastic wrap and refrigerate. Let the fish marinate for 3 to 4 hours.

3. In a large skillet, heat 1 tbsp of olive oil over medium-high heat until fragrant. Reduce the heat to medium and sauté the fillets, two or three at a time (depending on the size of your pan), for approximately 7 to 8 minutes, or to desired time, turning once about halfway through. Add additional olive oil between batches, as necessary.

4. Serve immediately with *moros* and *plátanos maduros*.

# Camarones Enchilados

(SHRIMP CREOLE)

⸺∞⸺

Camarones enchilados, *our name for shrimp creole, is one of my favorite foods. I like it because it's truly* comida criolla, *the traditional Cuban cuisine we created on the island and that Cubans eat every day. It has a sofrito, made with garlic and tomato sauce, that gives the shrimp just the right flavor.*

*One of the things I like most about typical Cuban foods like* camarones enchilados *is that you don't have to use a lot of seasonings or spices, because everything is simple and made with the things that grew naturally on the island.*

*As you've probably figured out by now, the basic ingredients in Cuban cuisine are just garlic, onion, and lime (or bitter orange). Add tomato sauce and cooking wine, and you have the* sofrito *that gives* camarones enchilados *their characteristic flavor, and reminds me of my childhood every time I smell it.*

—*Emilio*

⸺∞⸺

## YIELD: 4 SERVINGS

1 15-oz can tomato sauce

¼ tsp salt

¼ tsp dried oregano

pinch of cumin powder

¼ cup olive oil

½ large white onion, finely chopped

2 cloves garlic, minced

½ green pepper, cored, seeded, and finely chopped

¼ cup *vino seco* or dry white wine

1 cup pimento-stuffed olives

3 lbs large shrimp, shelled and deveined

CAMARONES ENCHILADOS

1. In a small bowl, whisk the tomato sauce, salt, oregano, and cumin.

2. To make the *sofrito* used in this dish, heat the olive oil in a large skillet over medium-high heat until just fragrant. Add the onions and cook for 1 to 2 minutes. Then add the garlic and green pepper. Stirring, cook for an additional 1 to 2 minutes or until the onions are translucent. Deglaze the *sofrito* by adding the *vino seco*, stirring gently. Add the tomato sauce mixture into the pan, bring the sauce to a simmer, and then reduce the heat to medium-low. Add the olives and allow the sauce to simmer gently for about 15 minutes.

3. Add the shrimp and cook in the sauce for 5 to 6 minutes or until the shrimp are fully cooked through, stirring occasionally and flipping the shrimp about halfway through using tongs.

4. Serve each portion in a small casserole dish with a generous helping of sauce.

### Tip from the Kitchen

This dish is best served over white rice. Just before serving, place about a cup of hot rice in each casserole dish. Then ladle the shrimp and sauce over the rice to cover completely.

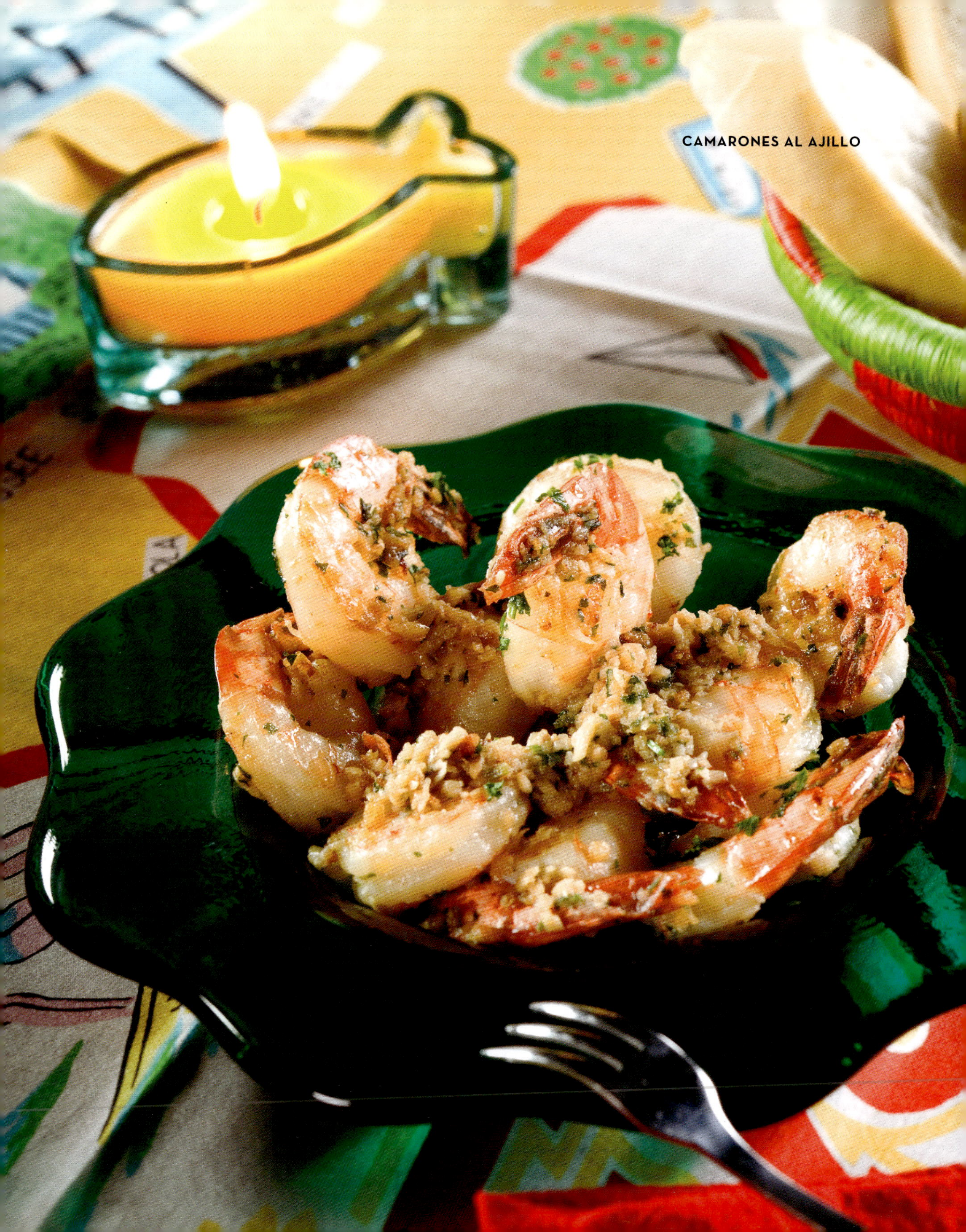
CAMARONES AL AJILLO

# Camarones al Ajillo

## (SHRIMP IN GARLIC SAUCE)

⌘

Camarones al ajillo *is exactly what its name says it is: shrimp in garlic sauce. It's simple, quick to make, and one of the best and most traditional ways to cook shrimp. From refrigerator to serving plate only takes about ten minutes.*

*The flavor comes from the garlic, wine, and olive oil, which the shrimp absorbs as it cooks.*

*You don't want much competing with the rich, garlicky taste, so this dish is most often served simply with white rice.*

*—Emilio*

⌘

### YIELD: 4 SERVINGS

1 cup olive oil

3 lbs large shrimp, shelled and deveined and tails removed

6 cloves garlic, finely sliced

1 cup *vino seco* or dry white wine

1 tsp salt

1/4 tsp oregano

pinch of cumin powder

4 parsley sprigs

1. In a large skillet, heat the olive oil over medium heat until fragrant. Add the shrimp and garlic and sauté until the shrimp starts to turn pink (about 4 to 5 minutes), turning the shrimp once using tongs.

2.  Reduce the heat to low. Add the wine, salt, oregano, and cumin, and cook for another 4 to 5 minutes.

3.  Using tongs, remove the shrimp from the pan, pour the sauce over the shrimp, garnish with parsley, and serve with white rice.

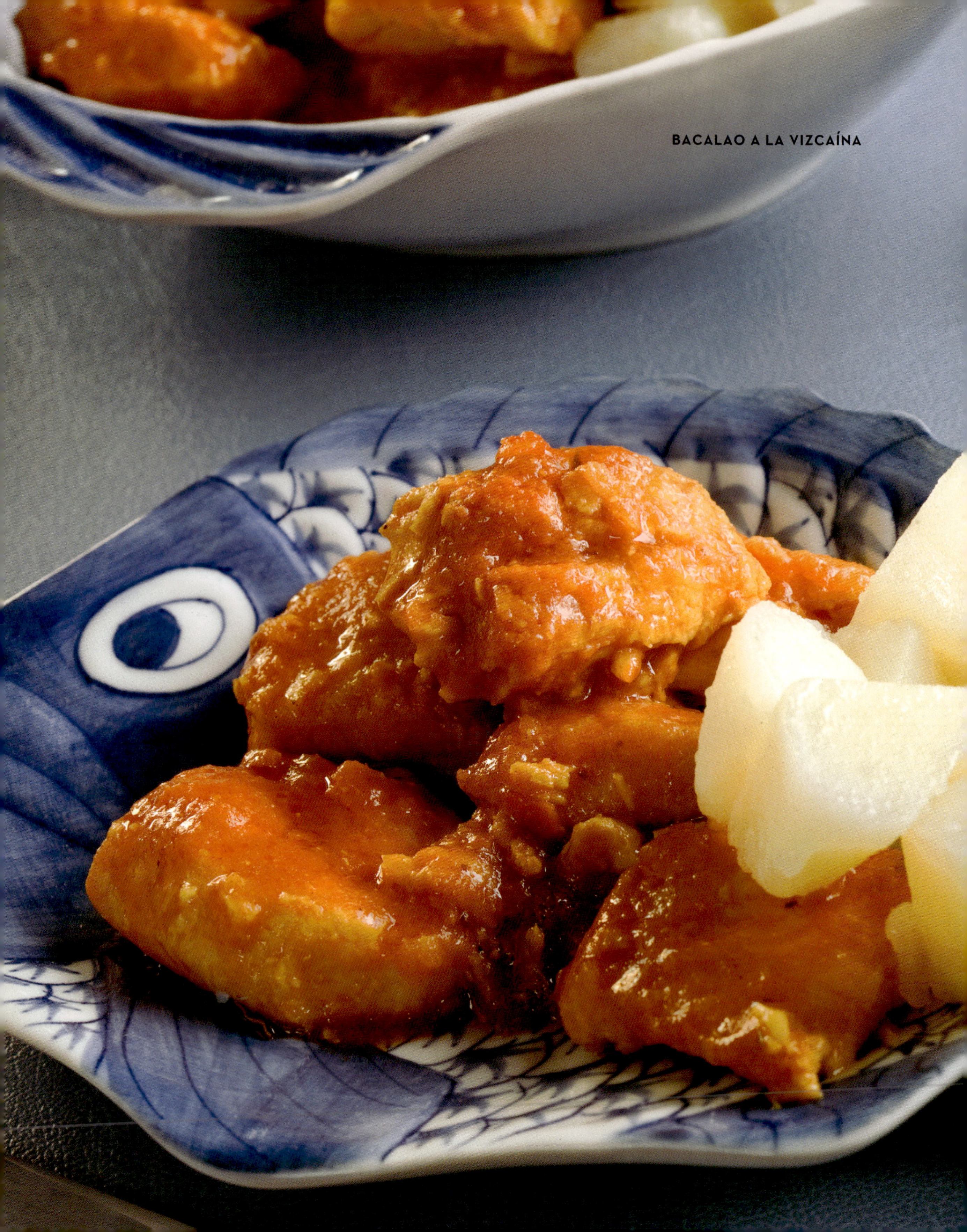
BACALAO A LA VIZCAÍNA

# Bacalao a la Vizcaína

## (CODFISH IN TOMATO SAUCE)

———✺———

I love bacalao a la vizcaína *because of the delicious tomato-based sauce. It's similar to the stew sauce in* carne con papas *and the Creole sauce in* camarones enchilados.

*But it's also one of my favorites because I love codfish. Bacalao is actually codfish cured in salt to preserve it. You have to soak it in water overnight so it will regain its moisture and the soaking removes a lot of the salt used in the curing process.*

*Cod has a flavor unlike any other fish. It's low in fat and high in protein. And when it's cooked a la vizcaína, it mixes with the garlic and tomato to create a dish that even people who aren't fish lovers can fall in love with.*

—Gloria

———✺———

### YIELD: 4 SERVINGS

2 lbs dried *bacalao* (salt-cured codfish)

water

5 oz olive oil

1 large onion, peeled and diced

1 large green pepper and 1 large red pepper, cored, seeded, and diced

2 cloves garlic, crushed (using a garlic press or mortar and pestle)

1/2 cup *vino* seco or dry white wine

1 15-oz can tomato sauce

1/4 tsp dried oregano

1 bay leaf

1. Rinse the *bacalao* under cool water for 5 to 10 minutes. Place the *bacalao* in a baking dish, and cover it with water and soak overnight in the refrigerator. Change the water once or twice if you want to further reduce the salt content. Drain the *bacalao*, then rinse it under cool running water for 10 to 15 minutes, then pat dry with paper towels. Separate the *bacalao* into bite-sized pieces.

2. Prepare a *sofrito* that will be used as a base for this dish. In a medium skillet, heat the olive oil over medium-high heat until fragrant. Then add the onions, the green and red peppers and garlic, then stir-fry for 3 to 4 minutes, until the onions are translucent.

3. Reduce the heat to medium-low and add the *bacalao*, followed by the *vino seco*, tomato sauce, oregano, and bay leaf. Bring the mixture to a gentle boil. Then reduce the heat to low, cover, and simmer for 20 minutes.

4. Serve with white rice and *plátanos maduros*.

CHULETAS DE PUERCO

# Chuletas de Puerco

(CUBAN-STYLE PORK CHOPS)

⎯⎯⎯⎯⎯⎯⎯⎯

Cubans love pork. We eat a lot of it, and not just the roasted variety we cook on special occasions. Pork chops are a regular favorite. They're quick and easy to make, and they have a taste that's out of this world.

The thing that makes Cuban-style pork chops special is the mojo, our extreme garlic-and-lime sauce. Marinate in the mojo for about thirty minutes, and you've turned plain pork chops into a tropical treat.

It's important to cover the chops when you cook them. Otherwise they can dry out in the pan. Keeping the cover on keeps them moist. When you remove the lid, you can turn up the heat and make the edges of the meat nice and crispy.

*—Gloria*

⎯⎯⎯⎯⎯⎯⎯⎯

**YIELD: 4 SERVINGS**

8 pork chops, about ½" thick

salt

2 cloves garlic, crushed (using a garlic press or mortar and pestle)

1 cup *mojo* (see recipe on page 159)

pinch of cumin powder

pinch of black pepper

olive oil for sautéing

1 medium onion, peeled and thinly sliced into rings

1. Pierce the pork chops with a fork (3 or 4 pierces per chop). Place the pork chops in a deep baking dish in a single layer, and sprinkle them with salt on both sides. Then rub the crushed garlic all over them. Pour the *mojo* over the

pork and top off with cumin and black pepper. Cover the dish with plastic wrap, and refrigerate for at least 6 hours or overnight.

2. In a large skillet with a lid, heat about 2 tablespoons of olive oil over medium-high heat until fragrant. Place 3 to 4 chops at a time into the heated oil and cook for 4 to 5 minutes per side or until pork is cooked through, keeping the lid on while cooking. Once the pork is cooked through, remove the lid, turn the heat up, and brown the edges of the chops a bit. Remove the chops and set aside. (Add olive oil between batches, as necessary.)

3. Once all the pork chops are cooked, remove the pan from the stove and wipe it with a paper towel. Add 2 tablespoons of olive oil, and heat it over medium-high heat. Sauté the onions in the pan for about 4 to 5 minutes or until they start to brown slightly. Pour the sautéed onions over the pork chops and serve immediately.

*Sides*

NAYIB ESTEFAN WITH HIS GRANDMOTHER NENA

*A* CUBAN MEAL WITHOUT side dishes would be like a sandwich without bread. It just wouldn't be a meal. When we say sides, we're referring to meal staples like plantains, *yuca*, or rice and beans.

What Americans do with potatoes, Cubans do with plantains. We fry them, mash them, and boil them. Plantains, though, will give you completely different tastes, from salty to sweet, depending on how ripe they are. You can do anything with plantains; and they really add a nice touch to any meal. The riper plantains are, the sweeter they are. The green banana is crunchy and salty.

Some people prefer *tostones.* Some people prefer *plátanos maduros.* I love them both. We Cubans like having that little sweet something mixed with every bite. And I've known many a Cuban who will just eat a sliced banana with their food, when they don't have plantains. Some people find it odd, but for us it's natural.

If you don't see plantains at the table, then we're probably serving *yuca. Yuca* was one of the native foods the Spaniards found already growing on the island. It's a starchy tuber that can be another substitute for potatoes in a Cuban meal, although we're not as likely to have *yuca* every day. It's a standard part of our traditional *Noche Buena* (Christmas Eve) feast. By itself, it's pretty bland, but boiled slowly and served covered with *mojo*, it's delicious.

With the obvious exceptions of *arróz con pollo* and *paella*, no Cuban dinner is complete without white rice and, usually, black beans. That's true *comida criolla*, and a mix of our Spanish and native roots.

The Spaniards took to them quickly, and used their traditional cooking styles to make black beans a uniquely Cuban dish. We pour them over the rice to mix the flavors together. Or you can cook them together with the rice to create a drier version called *moros*. Cooked together like that, the black beans tinge the rice with their flavor and coloring to create a unique texture and taste.

Black beans are a regular part of daily dinners. You'd be hard pressed to find a Cuban meal that doesn't include black beans.

We've gathered up some of our favorite traditional sides in this section. Feel free to mix and match them, like we do, to come up with the combinations you like best. There are no rules about what goes together. It's your own personal taste.

—*Gloria*

TOSTONES CON MOJO

# Tostones con Mojo

(GREEN PLANTAINS WITH GARLIC DRESSING)

❧

Tostones *are great. They're made from green plantains, peeled and cut cross-wise, the same as you slice a banana to put on cereal.*

Tostones *are fried twice. The first time is after you take the green plantain, peel it and cut it into little round chunks. Then you take them out of the oil and put them in a plantain press called a* tostonera, *but you can use other methods to flatten them out. My grandmother sometimes would use two saucers. Or she would do it with her own hands between pieces of cheesecloth.*

*One of the secrets I learned from my grandma about making tostones is to dip them in salted water after you fry them the first time. Then put them back in the oil to fry a second time. They turn out so crispy and are really, really delicious. If you decide to try my grandma's method, be extremely careful when you refry the soaked plantains, as droplets of water will cause the hot oil to spatter.*

—Gloria

❧

**YIELD: 4 SERVINGS**

| | |
|---|---|
| **2 large green plantains** | **salt** |
| **vegetable oil** | **½ cup *mojo* (see recipe on page 159)** |

1. Peel the plantains and cut cross-wise into 1" slices.

2. Fill a large skillet with vegetable oil to about ½" from the bottom and heat the oil over medium-high heat to 365°F.

3. Using tongs, carefully add the plantain slices to the heated oil in a single layer. Fry for about 3 to 4 minutes per side or until they start to take on a golden color. Carefully remove the plantains, and place them on a plate lined with paper towels to absorb excess oil. Reduce the heat to low, or if the rest of your dinner is not ready, turn off the stove.

4. Let the *tostones* cool for 5 minutes. Then, using a *tostonera* or by placing the plantain chunks between two saucers, flatten them to ¼" thickness.

5. Heat vegetable oil to 385°F over medium-high heat.

6. Once oil is at the proper temperature, using tongs, add the *tostones* back to the skillet in a single layer (you may need to work in batches) and fry for an additional 3 or 4 minutes until they turn a deep golden color.

7. Remove the *tostones* and transfer them to a plate lined with paper towels to absorb excess oil. Sprinkle with salt, to taste, transfer to a serving plate, and serve hot with *mojo* in a dipping bowl with a spoon for drizzling.

### Tip from the Kitchen

Some folks—let's call them "plantain purists"—prefer their *tostones* without the *mojo*, and these scrumptious tropical delights are certainly good enough without a dipping sauce. So, if you don't have time to make the *mojo* or don't care for garlic, just serve them salted.

# Plátanos Maduros

(FRIED SWEET PLANTAINS)

—※—

We use green plantains to make tostones, and ripe ones to make plátanos maduros.

Unlike the green ones, ripe plantains only get fried once. They're delicious that way, but for people like me who don't eat a lot of fried food, I have a great way of making a low-calorie version that's really quick.

I call them "nuclear plantains." What I do is take a really ripe plantain, cut off the ends, slice it down one side, and roll it up in wax paper like a Tootsie Roll. I make the wrap a little loose to give the plantain some room to grow, and then I zap it in the microwave for a minute and a half.

You don't have to put anything on that thing. Since you don't boil it, you don't boil out the taste. There's enough sugar in a plantain that it tastes great without having to fry it. It's got to be really ripe, though. It's a great alternative to a traditional Cuban favorite.

—Gloria

—※—

## YIELD: 4 SERVINGS

**2 large very ripe (heavily spotted or almost completely black skin) plantains**        **vegetable oil**

1. Peel the plantains, and cut them on the diagonal into slices of about ¾" in thickness.

PLÁTANOS MADUROS

2. In a deep skillet, add enough vegetable oil to come up about 1" from the bottom. Heat the oil over medium-high heat to 365°F.

3. Using a slotted spoon, carefully add the plantain slices (2 or 3 at a time) into the skillet. Try to keep them in a single layer, but some sticking will occur. Cook the plantains for approximately 2 minutes, stirring and turning occasionally. Then reduce the heat to medium-low, and continue cooking until the plantains are caramelized and turn a deep golden brown.

4. Carefully remove the plantains using a slotted spoon, and transfer them to a plate lined with paper towels to absorb excess oil. Serve warm.

## Tip from the Kitchen

If you're watching your weight, you might consider this "healthier" alternative to the fried version. It's nearly as tasty as the original and lower in fat and calories. You will need 2 large very ripe (heavily spotted or almost completely black skin) plantains, some wax paper, and a microwave oven.

1. Cut both ends off the plantains, and make a slit down the middle (lengthwise) of each plantain.

2. Wrap each plantain loosely in wax paper.

3. Place the plantains on a microwave-safe dish, and cook for 1½ minutes on high.

4. Let the plantains sit for 3 or 4 minutes, then peel them, and cut on the diagonal into slices about 1" thick and serve.

**FRIJOLES NEGROS**

# Frijoles Negros

## (BLACK BEANS)

———❧———

**F**ew things are as truly Cuban as black beans. The Taino natives who lived in Cuba cultivated and ate black beans long before Christopher Columbus sailed across the Atlantic and "discovered" them.

But it took Spanish and African influences to turn black beans into the traditional Cuban dish we know as frijoles negros today.

We like our beans nice and tender, and unlike the way the island natives made them, we add dry cooking wine to give them a distinctive flavor.

What gives Cuban black beans their unique taste, though, is the sofrito, a sautéed blend of onions, garlic, and green pepper. No Cuban meal is complete without a side of black beans.

—Emilio

———❧———

### YIELD: 8 TO 10 SERVINGS

1 lb black beans

10 cups water

1 large green bell pepper, cored, seeded, and halved

5 cloves garlic, 4 of them crushed (using a garlic press or mortar and pestle)

2/3 cup olive oil

1 bay leaf

3/4 tsp oregano

salt to taste

cumin powder to taste (optional)

1/2 cup *vino seco* or dry white wine

2 tbsp red wine vinegar (optional)

1. Rinse the beans thoroughly and remove any debris. Place the rinsed beans in a large covered pot or Dutch oven. Add the water, cover, and let sit overnight or for at least 6 hours.

2. Set stove to medium high and bring the beans to a boil. Add one of the green pepper halves, one of the onion halves, and a garlic clove. Cover and reduce heat to low, and cook for 45 to 60 minutes or until the beans become tender.

3. Meanwhile, finely chop the remaining halves of the green pepper and onion to be used in the *sofrito* that will be added to the beans for flavoring. In a large skillet, heat the olive oil over medium-high heat until fragrant. Then add the chopped onions and crushed garlic, and stir-fry for 3 to 4 minutes, until the onions are translucent. Add the chopped green pepper and cook for another 2 minutes, stirring constantly. Remove the pan from the heat.

4. Once the beans are tender (see step 2), fold the bean-*sofrito* mixture into the rest of the beans, and add the bay leaf, oregano, salt, cumin powder (if desired), and *vino seco.* Cover and allow the beans to simmer for another 30 to 45 minutes. If desired, stir in the vinegar during the last 10 to 15 minutes. (If you prefer "thicker" beans, uncover the beans during the last 10 to 15 minutes of cooking, but stay close and keep an eye on them so as not to end up with black bean cake!)

5. Remove and discard the bay leaf. Serve the beans piping hot over white rice.

ARRÓZ BLANCO

# Arróz Blanco

(WHITE RICE)

—⟨∞⟩—

Cubans like long-grain white rice generally slightly drier and more separated than the sticky steamed style the Chinese make. This is our primary starch staple, and it's impossible to imagine a dinner that doesn't include rice in one form or another.

Even the yellow rice you see with chicken in arróz con pollo is really white rice with a touch of Bijol powder or saffron added to give it that golden color.

As particular as we are about how our rice is made, we rarely eat it alone. We might pour red or black beans over it, mix it with the sauce from the main course, or cook it together with the beans to make moros or congrí, but we almost never eat rice all by itself. Some people even like a serving of white rice with a fried egg on it for breakfast.

So, if you're going to serve a truly Cuban meal, you have to include rice (and beans too!).

—Emilio

—⟨∞⟩—

## YIELD: 4 SERVINGS

2 cups long-grain white rice

3 cups water

1 tbsp olive oil

1 tsp salt

1. Rinse the rice thoroughly by placing it into a strainer and running cool water over it.

2. Place the rinsed rice in a large saucepan; then add the olive oil, water, and salt.

3. Bring to a boil over medium-high heat. Stir once, cover, reduce the heat to low, and cook for 20 minutes. Do not remove the cover! When the 20 minutes are up, remove the pan from the stove, and let it sit for 5 to 10 minutes. Fluff the rice using a fork and serve immediately.

# Moros

(MOORISH RICE [WHITE RICE COOKED WITH BLACK BEANS])

A meal without rice is practically unimaginable for Cubans. And one of our favorite ways of making it is to cook the beans and the rice together.

If you like a wetter mix of beans and rice, you'll prefer regular white rice with the black beans poured over it. But if you like your rice a little drier, moros is the way to go. There's a different taste to it, because the rice absorbs the taste of the black beans. It's delicious, but it's a totally different texture and taste.

With moros, the rice comes out fluffy, and since it's cooked with beef or chicken stock and chopped-up bacon, it has a meaty or smoky flavor you don't get with frijoles negros.

Of course, you can also make a vegetarian version using vegetable stock instead of the beef or chicken stock and eliminating the bacon. It's just delicious.

—Gloria

1 lb black beans (uncooked)

6 cups water

3 cups long-grain white rice

2 tbsp olive oil

2 tbsp vegetable oil

2 slices of bacon, finely chopped

1 large white onion, peeled and finely chopped

1 large green bell pepper, cored, seeded, and quartered

3 cloves garlic, crushed (using a garlic press or mortar and pestle)

4½ cups beef or chicken (or vegetable) stock

1 tsp salt

½ tsp freshly ground black pepper

1 tsp oregano

¼ tsp cumin powder

1 bay leaf

### Tip from the Kitchen

To make a "vegetarian" version of this dish, exclude the bacon and use vegetable stock instead of beef or chicken stock.

1. Rinse the beans thoroughly and remove any debris. Place the rinsed beans in a large saucepan. Add the water and bring to a boil over medium-high heat. Reduce the heat to low, cover, and cook beans for about 60 minutes or until the beans are tender. Drain using a strainer or colander.

2. Meanwhile, rinse the rice thoroughly by placing it into a strainer and running cool water over it. Set the rice aside and allow excess water to drain and the rice to dry for approximately 15 to 20 minutes.

3. Once the beans are tender and their cooking water has been drained, heat the olive oil together with the vegetable oil over medium-high heat in a large covered stockpot or Dutch oven. Add the bacon and sauté for 2 to 3 minutes. Then add the onions and green pepper and continue to sauté for an additional 3 or 4 minutes or until the onions are translucent. Add the garlic and the

rinsed rice and sauté for another 2 minutes, ensuring that the rice is evenly coated by the *sofrito*.

4. Add the beef stock or chicken stock, salt, pepper, oregano, cumin powder, and bay leaf, and bring the mixture to a boil, stirring occasionally.

5. Reduce the heat to low, cover, and simmer for 20 minutes. Remove the cover and taste the rice to make sure it is fully cooked. If the rice is not fully cooked, re-cover and cook for another 5 to 10 minutes.

6. Remove and discard the bay leaf and green pepper quarters and serve hot.

YUCA CON MOJO

# Yuca con Mojo

(YUCA WITH MOJO)

———— ❧ ————

Yuca was another one of those typically Cuban foods that the native Tainos grew and ate long before the first Spaniards landed on the island.

It's a starchy root vegetable with brown skin and white flesh that we eat instead of potatoes. Yuca is something we serve on special occasions, and as a standard part of our traditional Noche Buena (Christmas Eve) feast.

Getting fresh yuca just right is tricky, even for experienced Cuban cooks. Frozen yuca tends to turn out more consistently tender and perfect, so you might try that instead.

Sometimes we use a method called "scaring the yuca" in order to make it more tender. When it's boiling for a while and starting to soften, we throw in cold water to "scare" it; then let it boil again.

Yuca by itself is pretty plain and really starchy, but when smothered in mojo, it's delicious. However, it's really important to use the right mojo for yuca. The one we use is slightly different from the one we use on roast pork. With yuca we use naranja agria (sour orange) juice and salt, just like always, but we lightly sauté the garlic in olive oil before we pour the mixture over the vegetable. The mojo brings out the flavor of the yuca without overpowering it, and gives it a nice garlicky taste.

—Emilio

———— ❧ ————

2 lbs *yuca*

2 quarts water

1 tsp salt

1 cup ice water

**MOJO:**

3 oz *naranja agria* (sour orange) juice

½ tsp salt

2 tbsp olive oil

6 cloves garlic, crushed (using a garlic press or mortar and pestle)

**NOTE: The *mojo* for this dish is different from our regular *Mojo Criollo* recipe.**

1. Peel and thoroughly clean the *yuca*. Then cut it into chunks (about 2" to 3" in length).

2. Pour the water and salt into a large saucepan, and bring the water to a boil. Add the *yuca*, and bring the water to a boil a second time. Then reduce the heat to low, and cook, uncovered, for approximately 15 to 20 minutes or until the *yuca* begins to crack open.

3. Add the ice water and cook for an additional 5 to 10 minutes or until the *yuca* opens up and is fork tender. (If the *yuca* doesn't open on its own, you can use a fork to help the process.) Drain the *yuca*, and remove any fibers from the center.

4. In a medium bowl, gently whisk the *naranja agria* (you can substitute *naranja agria* juice with 2 parts lemon juice to 1 part orange juice in any recipe in this cookbook) and salt. Set aside.

5. In a small saucepan, heat the olive oil over medium heat until fragrant. Then add the garlic. Sauté the garlic for 1 minute, and remove it from the heat immediately. (For this dish, the garlic should not be browned.) Allow to cool for 2 minutes. Then pour the heated olive oil–garlic mixture into the *naranja agria*–salt blend and whisk.

6. Pour the warm *mojo* over the *yuca* and serve.

## Tip from the Kitchen

Achieving the right tenderness when using fresh *yuca* is tricky, even for seasoned Cuban-cuisine cooks. You might consider using frozen *yuca*, available in most Latin markets. The frozen variety turns out just right every time!

MOJO CRIOLLO

# Mojo Criollo

## (CREOLE MARINADE)

———⋙⋘———

**M**ojo criollo *is our extreme garlic sauce, and the secret ingredient that makes so many of our dishes special.*

It's an absolute must for roast pork and pan con lechón *sandwiches, and it's the perfect dipping sauce for plantain chips and Cuban steak fries made of yuca.*

*Unlike so many of our sofritos, which use lime or tomatoes or both to add a special sautéed flavor to our dishes,* mojo criollo *relies on sour orange, what we call* naranja agria, *to give it a citrus flavor.*

*That's another flavor we owe to our Arabian influences, by way of the conquistadores. The Moors were the first to introduce the sour orange to Spain. The Spaniards brought it with them to the New World, along with their cooking technique of using it as a marinade on fish and meat. In Cuba we added garlic, and decided that the new Creole concoction could be used on a range of foods, including plantains and yuca.*

—*Gloria*

———⋙⋘———

## YIELD: APPROXIMATELY 1 CUP MOJO

10 to 12 garlic cloves

2 tsp salt

1/2 tsp black pepper

1 tsp dried oregano

3/4 cup *naranja agria* (sour orange) juice

1/4 cup olive oil

1. In batches of about 6 cloves, peel and mash the garlic using a mortar and pestle (or crush using a garlic press).

2. In a small bowl, combine the mashed garlic with the salt, pepper, and oregano.

3. Stir in the *naranja agria* juice (you can substitute *naranja agria* juice with 2 parts lemon juice to 1 part orange juice in any recipe in this cookbook) and olive oil.

### Tip from the Kitchen

*N*aranja agria is a special, very tart variety of oranges available at Latin markets.

# Sandwiches

EMILIO WITH DAUGHTER EMILY

SANDWICHES ARE AS much a part of typical Cuban lunch fare as they are of American. What makes them unique, though, is the bread. We use only two kinds: Cuban bread and *medianoche* bread (or sweet bread). Anything else just isn't Cuban!

Cuban bread is like French bread, but with a somewhat softer crust. It has a pale, flaky crust, with a characteristic split down the middle. That comes from a palm frond that the bakers set on the doughy loaves while they're being made. The center is tender, but not chewy.

When I was a kid, my grandmother's brother worked at a Cuban bakery. So, of course, anytime they needed help, I was there. And there is nothing more delicious than the smell of baking Cuban bread. What makes it great is the lard in the bread. Of course, anything that's fattening is fantastic!

We would slather butter on it and then dip it in *café con leché* for breakfast. Like with most breads, Cuban bread is best eaten fresh, right out of the oven.

*Medianoche* bread lives up to its descriptive name. It's sweeter than Cuban bread, and it is easily distinguished by its soft brown crust. Also, it stays fresh much longer than Cuban bread. You can use the exact same sandwich ingredients and get a totally different taste just by switching the sweet bread for Cuban bread.

Cuban bread is essential to the Cuban sandwich. It features pork, ham, and cheese layered thick on Cuban bread. Then it's pressed nearly flat on a hot grill known as *la plancha,* which means "iron," like a clothes iron. That's exactly what it does—presses the sandwich as thin as it can be.

For a sweeter, lighter version of the Cuban sandwich, we make *medianoche,* or "midnight," sandwiches. They use most of the same ingredients—ham, pork, cheese, and pickle—but, as I mentioned, the bread changes the taste completely.

*Medianoche* bread is also the key ingredient to what is a bona fide traditional sandwich that you won't find in any other culture—the Elena Ruz, named after its creator. This sandwich incorporates turkey, cream cheese and strawberry preserves for a totally unexpected mix of flavors. They may not seem like they should go together, but believe me, they do. The Elena Ruz is delicious!

One of my favorite sandwiches with Cuban bread is *pan con lechón.* This sandwich is also named by its ingredients: bread and roast pork. It sounds simple, but the way the bread soaks up the juices from the pork and *mojo* makes it spectacular. It's one of the most delicious leftovers sandwiches in the world.

All of our sandwiches are big and filling, so they're perfect for sharing. They also make great party food. You can slice them into mini-sandwiches the way you would cut up a giant sub for a group, and let folks build a sampler platter with their favorite ones. That's sure to make everybody happy.

—*Gloria*

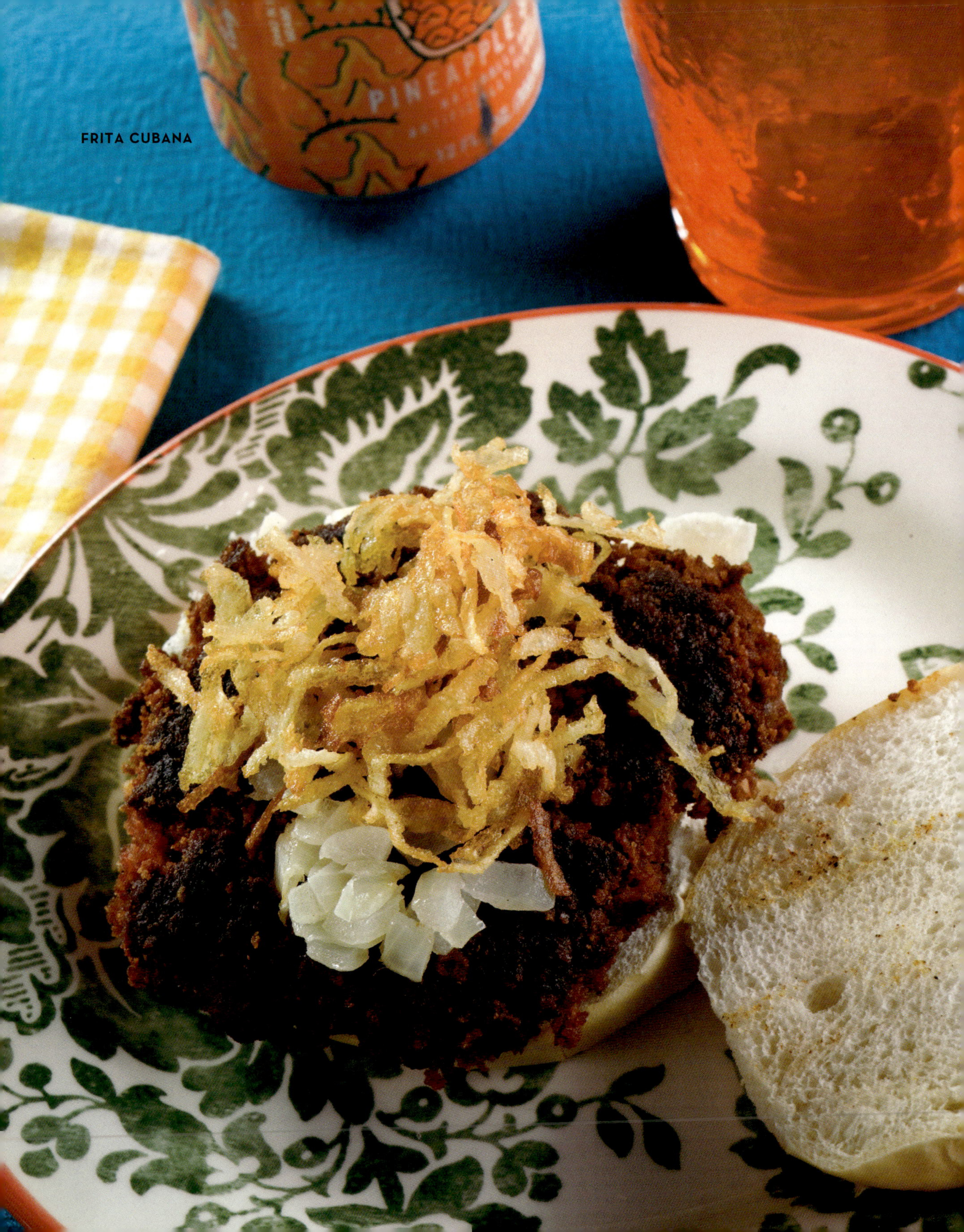

FRITA CUBANA

# Frita Cubana

(CUBAN HAMBURGER)

———❦———

In Cuba, papas fritas *means French fries, and* yuca frita *means cassava fries. But a* frita *can mean only one thing: that uniquely Cuban burger, the* frita cubana.

*We call it a Cuban hamburger, but it's really more than that. It has ground beef just like a regular American burger, but we mix in ground-up Spanish chorizo, along with some garlic, paprika, and vinegar. Then we form them into patties and toss them on the grill or into a skillet.*

*Most often we make them small, similar to the American "slider," but you can make them any size you like.*

*It's not just the mix of meats, the seasoning, or the size that makes them Cuban. We have a special way of serving them. Traditional Cuban style calls for topping them with shoestring potato sticks, before we put the top of the bun on. It adds a crunchy potato stick flavor to every bite, and a* frita *without them isn't a full-fledged Cuban burger.*

*—Emilio*

———❦———

2¹/2 lbs lean ground beef

¹/2 lb Spanish sausage, casings removed and ground

2 cloves garlic, peeled and minced

1 tbsp salt

1 tbsp paprika

¹/4 tsp cumin

2 oz white vinegar

vegetable oil or nonstick cooking spray

vegetable oil for sautéing

1 medium onion, finely chopped

8 hamburger buns

2 cans shoestring potato sticks

1. In a large bowl, combine the ground beef, ground chorizo, garlic, salt, paprika, cumin, and vinegar. Make 8 hamburger-style patties.

2. Lightly grease a large skillet with some vegetable oil or spray with nonstick cooking spray.

3. Working in batches of 2 or 3, cook the *fritas* over medium heat for 8 to 10 minutes or until fully cooked, flipping once. (The cooking time will vary depending on the thickness of your patties).

4. When the *fritas* are cooked, carefully wipe the skillet with paper towels, and heat 1 or 2 tablespoons of vegetable oil over medium heat. Then add the onions and sauté for 2 to 3 minutes until lightly browned.

5. Place a cooked *frita* on the bottom half of each bun and top with about a tablespoon of sautéed onion and a generous handful of potato sticks.

6. Serve immediately.

# Sándwich Cubano

(CUBAN SANDWICH)

———❧———

The Cuban sandwich is really a meal on a bun. It's huge. I actually have a hard time getting my mouth around one, unless it's pressed really, really flat.

The pressing is part of what makes the Cuban sandwich special. It doesn't just flatten the sandwich—it seals in the juices of the meat and melts the cheese. Most restaurants use a sandwich press, but you can use a meat press or heavy cast-iron pan to flatten the sandwich down at home. When you're done, the bread forms a stiff case that holds the sandwich together.

The bread is another crucial part of a true Cuban sandwich. It should be Cuban bread. You can use French bread if that's all you can find, but it won't be quite the same. Cuban bread gives it a flavor unlike other breads.

Then you load up the bread with thin slices of pork and ham, and top it with some Swiss cheese, mustard, and a slice of pickle. We pile everything in there. We tend to be excessive, so we pile on the food like we pile on the love.

The mark of a real Cuban sandwich is the way it's sliced. The traditional way is to slice it diagonally, from corner to corner, so the halves end up looking like long triangles.

—Gloria

———❧———

SÁNDWICH CUBANO

1 lb *lechón asado* (see recipe on page 99), sliced or shredded

1 lb sliced bolo ham

¾ lb Swiss cheese, sliced

2 large loaves Cuban or French bread

dill pickles, sliced

yellow mustard

1. Bring the sandwich meats and cheese to room temperature.

2. Cut the tips off the ends of your loaf. Then cut the bread into pieces about 8" or 9" in length. (You should easily get two pieces per loaf.) Slice the pieces in half.

3. Stack about ¼ lb of ham, 4 or 5 pickle slices (spread out evenly), 2 or 3 slices of Swiss cheese, and about ¼ lb *lechón* on each sandwich. Spread a light coat of yellow mustard on the inside of the top half of the bread.

4. Preheat your sandwich press (if you have one), a flat griddle, or a large skillet to medium heat.

5. Working with two sandwiches at a time, place the sandwiches in the press and close it. If you're using a griddle or skillet, place the sandwiches on the griddle or in the skillet, and place a heavy meat press or cast-iron pan on top of the sandwich. Press down to flatten the sandwich. Heat the sandwich for 5 to 6 minutes in the press or 2 to 3 minutes per side if using a griddle or skillet.

6. Slice the sandwiches in half lengthwise and serve hot.

### Tip from the Kitchen

*B*olo ham or other sweet ham should be used for this sandwich. Avoid using smoked ham, as this will overpower the other ingredients.

PAN CON LECHÓN

# Pan con Lechón

(CUBAN-STYLE ROASTED PORK SANDWICH)

※

There's nothing better than getting up on Christmas day and knowing that there's going to be pan con lechón. It's like turkey sandwiches the day after Thanksgiving. Pan con lechón is what we do with the leftovers from the roast pork we ate on Christmas Eve.

I'll never forget how my grandma would prepare the pork for those sandwiches. She would bone the pork and make sure there was nothing left but the meat and the crispy skin. Then she took a big cleaver and chopped it all up so that everything was bite-sized, and heated it all up in the oven. When it was nice and warm, she would take sautéed onions and mix it in with the pork, slap the mixture on a piece of Cuban bread, and pour on the mojo, and you'd have the most delicious pan con lechón in the world.

The bread is important. To make a truly traditional pan con lechón, use Cuban bread. It's perfect for a moist sandwich like pan con lechón because the soft center soaks up the mojo, but the firm crust keeps the natural juices from leaking out.

—Gloria

※

## YIELD: 4 SANDWICHES

2 large loaves Cuban or French bread

vegetable oil for sautéing

2 lbs *lechón asado* (see recipe on page 99), sliced or shredded

2 tbs *mojo criollo* (see recipe on page 159)

1 medium onion, thinly sliced

1. Cut the tips off the ends of your loaf. Then cut the bread into pieces about 8" or 9" in length. (You should easily obtain two pieces per loaf.) Slice the pieces in half.

2. In a large skillet, heat about a tablespoon of vegetable oil over medium heat. Then add the *lechón* and sauté for 1 to 2 minutes. Add the *mojo criollo* and continue to cook for another 2 to 3 minutes or until the meat is evenly heated.

3. Arrange approximately a half pound of the *lechón* on the bottom half of each sandwich loaf.

4. Preheat your sandwich press (if you have one), a flat griddle, or a large skillet to medium heat.

5. Working with two sandwiches at a time, place the sandwiches in the press and close it. If you're using a griddle or skillet, place the sandwiches on the griddle or in the pan, and place a heavy meat press or cast-iron pan on top of the sandwich and press down to flatten the sandwiches. Heat the sandwiches for 5 to 6 minutes in the press or 2 to 3 minutes per side if using a griddle or skillet.

6. Meanwhile, using the same skillet in which you heated the *lechón*, heat 1 or 2 tablespoons of vegetable oil over medium heat. Add the onions and sauté for 2 to 3 minutes, until lightly browned.

7. When the sandwiches are thoroughly heated, uncover each sandwich and top it off with a thin layer of the sautéed onions.

8. Slice the sandwiches in half on the diagonal and serve hot.

MEDIANOCHE

# Medianoche

### (MIDNIGHT SANDWICH)

———✺✺✺———

The ingredients in a medianoche are pretty much the same as what goes in a Cuban sandwich, but the bread gives it a totally different taste and texture. The medianoche has the same roasted pork and bolo ham as a Cuban sandwich, as well as the Swiss cheese, mustard, and pickle. But the medianoche uses sweet bread. That gives the medianoche a subtle sweetness that you don't find in the traditional Cuban sandwich.

It's also softer than a Cuban sandwich, which is why I, personally, like it better.

The medianoche is another one of those multipurpose Cuban foods. You can serve it as a meal by itself or with some fries or chips, or you can cut it into mini-sandwiches and serve it at a party the same way you would a sub or Cuban sandwich. They also sell sweet bread rolls that taste the same, but are smaller and easier to handle than the full-sized buns.

—Gloria

———✺✺✺———

## YIELD: 4 SANDWICHES

1 lb *lechón asado* (see recipe on page 99), sliced or shredded

1 lb bolo ham, sliced

3/4 lb Swiss cheese, sliced

4 *medianoche* sandwich rolls (or sweet hoagie rolls)

dill pickles, sliced

yellow mustard

1. Bring the sandwich meats and cheese to room temperature.

2. Slice each roll in half.

3. Stack about ¼ pound of ham, 4 or 5 pickle slices (spread out evenly), 2 or 3 slices of Swiss cheese, and about ¼ pound *lechón* on each sandwich. Spread a light coat of yellow mustard on the inside of the top half of the roll.

4. Preheat your sandwich press (if you have one), a flat griddle, or a large skillet to medium heat.

5. Working with two sandwiches at a time, place the sandwiches in the press and close it. If you're using a griddle or skillet, place the sandwiches on the griddle or in the pan, and place a heavy meat press or cast-iron pan on top of the sandwich and press down to flatten the sandwich. Heat the sandwich for 5 to 6 minutes in the press or 2 to 3 minutes per side if using a griddle or skillet.

6. Slice the sandwiches in half on the diagonal and serve hot.

SÁNDWICH ELENA RUZ

# Sándwich Elena Ruz

### (ELENA RUZ TURKEY SANDWICH)

⸎

An Elena Ruz sandwich is an odd mix of ingredients, things you might not think would go well together. But when you bite into it, it's a fantastic taste explosion.

It's like a Cuban sandwich version of turkey and cranberry sauce—a mix of salty and sweet flavors that come together to create a taste that's greater than the sum of the parts. And I don't know of any other sandwich that's quite like it.

Elena Ruz was a lady who went to a restaurant called El Carmelo in Havana. She asked the restaurant staff to make a sandwich by putting some turkey, cream cheese, and strawberry marmalade on a medianoche roll. And because she went there a lot and always asked for it, the owners put it on the menu and named it after her.

That's a true story. Her sister worked with me at Bacardi and she told me how it all started. Now the Elena Ruz is a classic Cuban-style sandwich.

*—Emilio*

⸎

## YIELD: 4 SANDWICHES

1 lb turkey breast, sliced

8 oz cream cheese, softened

4 *medianoche* sandwich rolls (or sweet hoagie rolls)

½ jar of strawberry preserves

1. Bring the sandwich meat and cream cheese to room temperature.

2. Slice each roll in half lengthwise.

3. Slather about 2 ounces of cream cheese on the bottom half of each roll and top with 2 to 3 tablespoons of strawberry preserves. Then spread the preserves over the cream cheese evenly.

4. Top the strawberry preserves with about ¼ pound of turkey on each sandwich.

5. Preheat your sandwich press (if you have one), a flat griddle, or a large skillet to medium heat.

6. Working with two sandwiches at a time, place the sandwiches in the press and close it. If you're using a griddle or skillet, place the sandwiches on the griddle or in the pan, and place a heavy meat press or cast-iron pan on top of the sandwich and press down to flatten the sandwich. Heat the sandwich for 3 to 4 minutes in the press or 1 to 2 minutes per side if using a griddle or skillet.

7. Slice the sandwiches in half on the diagonal and serve warm.

Desserts

EMILIO AND GLORIA

*I* ABSOLUTELY LOVE DESSERTS! But then again, who doesn't? I don't know if we have a genetic sweet tooth that requires it, but dinner without dessert feels incomplete. Emilio is one person who can't do without dessert after a meal.

Everyone has their own personal preference. Desserts don't have to be fancy. A slice of guava paste with cheese—what we call *timba*—will do. Many Cubans prefer guava to almost any other dessert. Emilio does. Guava has a special place in Cuban culture. The good thing is that, unlike many desserts, guavas are actually good for you. Guavas are often called "superfruit," because they're so rich in vitamins. A guava has more vitamin C than most other citrus fruits. In fact, the rind has more than five times as much vitamin C as an orange.

You can eat the whole guava—seeds, rind, and all—but usually we cut out the center, where all the seeds are packed in. The sweetest part of the pulp is in the center.

One of my favorite guava desserts is what we call *cascos de guayaba*, which is basically the peeled and cored meat of a couple of guavas in a heavy, sweet syrup. The syrup is made from sugar boiled in water until it thickens.

It's no wonder we use so much sugar in our desserts. Sugarcane was always one of the principal crops in Cuba, so sugar is one thing we always had plenty of. And it's an essential ingredient in all of our desserts.

I have to admit that when most people think of Cuban desserts, though, they think of *flan*. And they're right. It is quintessentially Cuban, even though there are variations of it all over the world. The European version is known by the French name, *crème caramel*. But to Cubans it's *flan*, and it's as much a part of our culture as mambo music.

My favorite dessert is *flan de queso*, *flan* made with cream cheese. It's almost like a cheesecake *flan*. The creamy inside is very sweet and then again a little tart, with slightly scorched caramel on the outside. It's a mouthwatering combo! Another variation that brings together two of our favorite dessert dishes is the *flan de guayaba y queso*, the guava-and-cheese flan. That's perfect for people who can't decide which they like better for dessert. It's the best of both worlds.

The other two traditional desserts are *arróz con leche* (rice pudding), and *natilla*, a custard sort of like crème brûlée, but without the hard caramel topping. And just like pie, *arróz con leche* is a natural finish to a meal. *Arróz con leche* and *natilla* were the best ways for Cuban grandmothers to show off their cooking abilities, and fatten up us "skinny" kids. Like many desserts, there are *natilla* variations throughout all of Latin America, but we're proud of our Cuban style, with some cinnamon on top, and plenty of eggs and sugar within.

The recipes in this section are all of our favorite traditional desserts, along with variations that will keep every sweet tooth in your family satisfied. But be warned: They're addictive!

—*Gloria*

# *Flan*

❦

ood flan *has to have the right consistency. It has to be creamy—not too thick, not too watery, not lumpy at all. And that's all about the eggs.*

*You have to use lots of eggs. You can't scrimp on that. Some people cut corners and don't put as many yolks in it as they should, and the flan suffers. I say: If you're going to have it, have it all the way.*

*Flan has to be slow cooked, and the caramel needs to be made slowly so that you don't burn it. Unlike crème brûlée, which falls over if you remove the hard caramel crust, flan stands on its own.*

*Cubans love flan so much we've come up with all kinds of variations. There's the traditional version, which is a simple, sweet, savory custard with that vaguely tart, slightly scorched caramel on the outside. There's* flan de chocolate *for chocolate lovers,* flan de mango, *and just about every other tropical fruit flavor you can think of. The* flan de guayaba y queso, *the guava-and-cheese flan, is delicious. But my favorite is the* flan de queso, *because it's almost like a cheesecake flan.*

*Try them all, and find your favorite. Or experiment with the recipes, using flavors you like, and come up with a flan that's all your own.*

—Gloria

❦

FLAN

# Flan Tradicional

(TRADITIONAL FLAN)

## YIELD: 8 TO 10 SERVINGS

1 cup plus 1 tbsp granulated sugar

6 large egg yolks

3 large eggs

1 14-oz can sweetened condensed milk

1 12-oz can evaporated milk

1 cup whole milk

¼ tsp salt

1 tsp vanilla extract

1. Heat the granulated sugar in a medium heavy-bottom saucepan over medium heat without stirring until the sugar starts to melt and turn a golden color along the edges of the pan. (**Note: You must stay near the stove at all times and pay close attention to make sure sugar doesn't burn.**) Reduce the heat to medium and swirl the saucepan to cover the bottom evenly. Continue to heat the sugar, swirling the pan constantly, until it caramelizes and the caramel takes on a golden brown color. Remove from heat and immediately pour an even amount into each of ten ramekins (or a 2-quart ovenproof mold). Using oven mitts or a hot pad to grab the ramekins (or mold) and working quickly so the caramel doesn't harden, swirl the ramekins (or mold), making sure the bottom of each is covered completely and the caramel goes up the sides a bit. Set aside.

2. Position a rack in the center of the oven and preheat the oven to 350°F.

3. Using an electric mixer set at the lowest speed, mix the egg yolks and eggs in a large bowl. Beat in the condensed milk, then the evaporated milk, then the whole milk. Using a wire whisk, gently fold in the remaining tablespoon of sugar, the salt, and the vanilla.

4. Slowly pour an equal amount of the custard into each of the ramekins. Using a wooden spoon, skim off any bubbles that form on top.

5. Transfer the ramekins to a baking dish filled with hot water that will rise two-thirds of the way up the sides of the ramekins once all ramekins are in the dish. Remove or add hot water as necessary as you add each ramekin.

6. Bake in the oven for 1 hour or until the centers of the flans are firm to the touch. (Cooking time will be 75 to 90 minutes if using a single mold.)

7. Place the ramekins on a wire rack and allow to cool to room temperature. Then refrigerate for at least 4 hours or overnight.

8. To unmold, run a sharp knife very carefully around the edge of each custard. Place a dessert plate on top of each ramekin, flip it over, and tap gently until the flan is loose. Remove the ramekin and serve chilled or at room temperature.

# Flan de Queso

(CREAM CHEESE FLAN [CUBAN-STYLE CHEESECAKE])

## YIELD: 8 TO 10 SERVINGS

| | |
|---|---|
| 1 cup granulated sugar | 8 oz cream cheese, softened |
| 1 12-oz can evaporated milk | 5 eggs |
| 1 14-oz can sweetened condensed milk | 1 tsp vanilla |

1. Heat the granulated sugar in a medium heavy-bottom saucepan over medium-high heat without stirring until the sugar starts to melt and turn a golden color along the edges of the pan. (**Note: You must stay near the stove at all times and pay close attention to make sure the sugar doesn't burn.**) Reduce the heat to medium, and swirl the saucepan to cover the bottom evenly. Continue to heat the sugar, swirling the pan constantly, until it caramelizes and the caramel takes on a golden brown color. Remove from heat and immediately pour an even amount into each of ten ramekins (or a 2-quart ovenproof mold). Using oven mitts or a hot pad to grab the ramekins (or mold), swirl the ramekins (or mold), making sure the bottom of each is covered completely and the caramel goes up the sides a bit. Set aside.

2. Position a rack in the center of the oven and preheat the oven to 350°F.

3. In a blender or food processor, mix the remaining ingredients just until smooth.

4. Slowly pour an equal amount of the flan mixture into each of the ramekins (or all of the mixture into the mold).

5. Place the ramekins (or mold) in a large roasting pan. Pour hot water into the roasting pan until it reaches two-thirds up the sides of the ramekins (or mold). Place roasting pan on the center rack, and bake for 60 minutes or until a knife inserted in the center comes out clean. (Cooking time will be 75 to 90 minutes if using a single mold.)

**6.** Place the ramekins on a wire rack and allow to cool to room temperature, then unmold by running a sharp knife very carefully around the edges of each custard. Place a dessert plate on top of each ramekin (or serving dish on top of the mold), flip it over, and tap gently until the flan is loose. Refrigerate for at least 4 hours or overnight, and serve chilled.

# Flan de Chocolate

(CHOCOLATE FLAN)

## YIELD: 8 TO 10 SERVINGS

1 cup plus 1 tbsp granulated sugar

6 large egg yolks

3 large eggs

1 14-oz can sweetened condensed milk

1 12-oz can evaporated milk

1 cup milk

¼ tsp salt

1 tsp vanilla extract

½ cup unsweetened cocoa powder

1. Follow the recipe for traditional flan (see recipe on page 189), but add ½ cup of unsweetened cocoa powder when making the flan mixture (add ¼ cup of cocoa powder between each milk addition).

**FLAN DE CHOCOLATE**

# Flan de Guayaba y Queso

(GUAVA-AND-CHEESE FLAN)

**YIELD: 8 TO 10 SERVINGS**

1 cup granulated sugar

1 12-oz can evaporated milk

1 14-oz can sweetened condensed milk

6 oz cream cheese, softened

5 eggs

1 tsp vanilla

6 oz guava marmelade*

1.  Follow the recipe for *flan de queso* (see page 191), but use only 6 ounces of cream cheese and add 6 ounces of guava marmelade to the flan mixture.

\* You can make your own guava marmelade if you are unable to find it in your market. Begin with a can of guava shells, drain about half of the syrup, then puree the remaining syrup and the shells in a blender or food processor until smooth. Pour the guava puree into a saucepan, then cook over medium heat for about 15 to 20 minutes. Let cool before mixing with other ingredients.

**FLAN DE GUAYABA Y QUESO**

ARRÓZ CON LECHE

# Arróz con Leche

(RICE PUDDING)

———⊗———

Arróz con leche *is one of my favorite desserts. The Cuban version is richer, sweeter, and tinged with a citrus taste.*

*One of the secrets of a good rice pudding is to use a little bit of citrus rind (orange or lemon) to give it a slightly bitter taste as well. Either way, the touch of sharply acidic citrus complements the sugar and cinnamon, and gives* arróz con leche *a completely traditional Cuban flavor.*

*—Emilio*

———⊗———

### YIELD: 6 TO 8 SERVINGS

1 cup short-grain (*Valencia*) rice, thoroughly rinsed

4 cups water

⅛ tsp salt

1 piece lemon or orange rind without any flesh (optional)

2 cinnamon sticks

3 cloves (optional)

2 cups whole milk

1 12-oz can evaporated milk

1 14-oz can sweetened condensed milk

1 tsp vanilla extract

cinnamon powder

1. Place the rice, water, and salt into a large (5-quart) pot or a casserole. Bring to a boil over medium heat. Add the lemon (or orange) rind, cinnamon sticks, and cloves, and reduce the heat to medium-low (just enough heat so the water is gently simmering). Cook the rice uncovered for approximately 30 to 45

minutes, or until the rice is tender and most of the water is absorbed. Remove the lemon rind, cinnamon sticks, and cloves.

2. Meanwhile, in a large bowl, lightly whisk the whole milk, evaporated milk, condensed milk, and vanilla. Once the rice is tender (see step 1), stir the milk mixture into the rice, reduce the heat to low and continue to cook over low heat, stirring occasionally, for 20 to 30 minutes, or until the rice pudding thickens to desired consistency.

### Tip from the Kitchen

The rice pudding will thicken more as it cools, so be careful not to overcook. The rice pudding should have a very creamy consistency. If yours doesn't, try reducing the cooking time the next time you make it.

3. Remove from heat, and let cool at room temperature.

4. Using a ladle, fill 8 to 10 custard cups with the pudding. Refrigerate until completely chilled, for at least 3 hours or overnight.

5. Dust with cinnamon powder (to taste) just before serving.

**PUDÍN DE PAN**

# Pudín de Pan

(CUBAN-STYLE BREAD PUDDING)

B read pudding is another one of those desserts that have been around for so long that their origins are lost in history. Most agree, however, that it came about thanks to frugal cooks who didn't want to waste bread that had gone stale.

Rather than throw it out, they soaked it in milk or cream, sweetened it, and baked it.

The way we make it, in the traditional Cuban style, uses vanilla and a cinnamon stick, along with a little light or dark Cuban rum. We also use a piece of lemon rind to give it a slightly tart flavor that harmonizes with the sugary sweetness. The rum and the rind combine to give our pudín de pan its traditional Cuban flavor.

—Emilio

## YIELD: 10 TO 12 SERVINGS

1¹/₂ cups granulated sugar

1 loaf white bread

1 quart milk

1 piece lemon rind (without any flesh)

1 cinnamon stick

¹/₄ tsp salt

6 eggs

2 tbsp light or dark rum (optional)

1 tsp vanilla

cinnamon, to taste

nutmeg, to taste

¹/₂ cup raisins

1. Heat ½ cup of the granulated sugar in a medium heavy-bottom saucepan over medium-high heat without stirring until the sugar starts to melt and turn a

golden color along the edges of the pan. **(Note: You must stay near the stove at all times and pay close attention to make sure the sugar doesn't burn.)** Reduce the heat to medium, and swirl the saucepan to cover the bottom evenly. Continue to heat the sugar, swirling the pan constantly to avoid scorching, until it caramelizes, and the caramel takes on a golden brown color. Remove it from the heat and pour it into a large loaf pan. Using oven mitts or a hot pad to grab the pan, carefully swirl the caramel in the loaf pan to completely coat the bottom and to partially glaze the sides of the pan with the caramel. Set the loaf pan aside.

2. Tear the bread into small pieces and place them in a large mixing bowl.

3. Place the milk, lemon rind, cinnamon stick, and salt in a medium (2-quart) saucepan, and bring the mixture to a boil over medium heat. As soon as the milk boils, remove it from the heat. Remove the cinnamon stick and lemon rind, and pour the heated milk over the bread pieces. Mix with a wooden spoon and set aside. Allow to cool for 15 minutes.

4. Preheat the oven to 350°F.

5. In a medium bowl, mix the eggs, the rum (if desired), the remaining cup of sugar, the vanilla, cinnamon powder, and the nutmeg thoroughly, then fold into the bread mixture. Add the raisins, and combine thoroughly.

6. Pour the bread-pudding mixture into the caramelized loaf pan and cover with heavy-duty aluminum foil, pinching along the edges of the pan to seal. Place the covered loaf pan in a large roasting pan. Pour hot water into the roasting pan until it reaches halfway up the sides of the covered loaf pan. Place the roasting pan on the center rack, and bake for an hour or until a toothpick inserted into the center comes out clean.

7. Remove from the oven and allow to cool completely. Then refrigerate for at least 4 hours or overnight.

8. When ready to serve, loosen the sides with a paring knife, place a deep serving dish on top of the loaf pan, and carefully invert the loaf pan to release the bread pudding and caramel sauce. Slice and serve. Spoon additional caramel on each serving, as desired.

# Natilla

⸻

Natilla *is a sweet custard dish like a crème brûlée without the sugar crust burned on top. Like many other desserts, variations of it exist around the world.*

*The Cuban style is similar to its Spanish ancestor, but once again, Cubans added their distinctive tropical touch to the original to come up with a recipe all their own.*

*Both use milk, sugar, eggs, vanilla, and cinnamon. And both are prepared by bringing the milk to a boil and mixing it in with the eggs. The result is similar to a rich flan, without the caramel.*

*But in the Cuban version, we add a piece of lemon rind to bring out the sugary sweetness of the custard and give it its characteristic taste.*

—Gloria

⸻

## YIELD: 8 SERVINGS

8 egg yolks

1 cup granulated sugar

4 tbsp cornstarch

3 cups whole and 1 cup evaporated milk

1 piece lemon rind (without any flesh)

1 cinnamon stick

1/4 tsp salt

1 1/2 tsp vanilla

cinnamon powder, to taste

1. In a large mixing bowl, using an electric (or stand) mixer on low speed, mix the egg yolks, sugar, and cornstarch until completely smooth. Then set aside.

2. Place the milk, the lemon rind, the cinnamon stick, and the salt in a medium (2½ quart) saucepan, and bring the mixture to a boil over medium-low heat, watching closely and stirring occasionally to avoid scorching the milk. As soon as the milk boils, remove it from the heat and allow to cool for approximately 5 minutes.

3. Remove the lemon rind and cinnamon stick from the milk. Then gradually pour the heated milk into the egg mixture, stirring constantly with a wooden spoon (or using the paddle attachment of a stand mixer set on low).

4. Return the custard mix to the same saucepan used to heat the milk.

5. Heat the custard over medium heat and bring to a boil, stirring constantly. Reduce the heat to low. Then cook for 2 to 3 minutes or until the pudding thickens to the desired consistency. Add the vanilla, stir, and remove from heat.

6. Using a ladle, fill eight custard cups. Let cool at room temperature for approximately 45 minutes. Refrigerate the *natilla* until completely chilled, for at least 3 hours or overnight.

7. Serve with a dusting of cinnamon powder.

CASCOS DE GUAYABA CON QUESO CREMA

# Cascos de Guayaba
# con Queso Crema

(GUAVA SHELLS WITH CREAM CHEESE)

———✸———

Guava has to be the number one fruit for Cubans. And one of the best ways to have it is drenched in a sugary syrup, with cream cheese.

Again, it's that mix of sweet and salty that makes it so phenomenal. Taste it, and you'll understand why.

But cascos de guayaba con queso crema isn't just one of the best-tasting desserts; it's one of the few desserts that you can say is actually good for you. (Although, with all that syrup and cheese, it's also high in calories.) Guavas are especially rich in vitamin C.

Cascos de guayaba con queso crema is one of the easiest desserts you can make, and a great choice for cooks who are pressed for time. It only takes a couple of minutes to prepare. All you need is a can of guava shells in heavy syrup and a package of cream cheese. Spoon out a couple of shells and cut a couple of slices of the cheese, and you're done. I love to eat it with saltines or Cuban crackers.

It's heavenly.

—Gloria

———✸———

**1 package of cream cheese**

**1 can guava shells in heavy syrup, chilled**

1. Slice the cream cheese into ½" slices.

2. Serve 2 to 3 guava shells with 2 to 3 slices of cream cheese. Drizzle some of the syrup over the plate.

# Beverages

ESTEFAN FAMILY

"Y *MOJITO* IN La Bodeguita del Medio, my daiquiri in El Floridita," wrote Cuba lover Ernest Hemingway, referring to two Havana restaurants that were among his favorite hangouts and two of Cuba's favorite drinks.

The endorsement of such a famous author may have helped popularize these drinks, but both are as typically Cuban as sugarcane and salsa dancing. Both use traditional Cuban ingredients—sugar and rum. Growing up near the Bacardi rum factory in Santiago, Cuba, I saw people drinking *mojitos* as far back as I can remember.

The *mojito* is a relative to the daiquiri, which shares the basic ingredients, minus the mint and club soda. Named after a town near the one where I grew up, the *daiquirí* was well known on the island.

Rum is, beyond doubt, Cuba's native liquor, and true Cuban drinks are made with rum. One of the simplest to make has a long history, but a particular significance for Cubans in the United States. *Cuba libre* means "a free Cuba," and while all it adds is a fresh squeeze of lime and a wedge to a basic rum and Coke, the name makes it special for Cuban exiles who long for the day Cuba will be free. It's one of the most popular rum drinks.

*Batidos,* Cuban milk shakes, are blended with papaya, mango, or mamey.

People often think of these fruits as exotic, but to Cubans, they're as common as oranges. They are the flavors of our homeland, and mixing them up into a uniquely tropical version of a smoothie yields a vitamin-packed and fragrant blend that carries me back to my childhood. I can see the mango trees full with the purple and green fruit, and I can see my mother cutting open the yellow-green papayas to reveal their ripe red interiors.

There's a smell and taste that signifies Cuba more than any other and that no Cuban can do without. In this section, we've included the most Cuban of the Cuban concoctions: *café cubano.*

For Cubans, no day begins without *café cubano,* and no meal ends without it. It isn't espresso, and it definitely isn't just "a cup of coffee." Cuban coffee is the true flavor of Cuba, in a cup. We drink it straight up, lightened with milk in *café con leche,* or added as a jolt of color and caffeine to top off a demitasse of evaporated milk.

Cuban coffee is a necessary final part for any traditional Cuban dinner. It's also perfect all by itself any time of the day, when you want a true taste of Cuba and a pick-me-up. No matter how you drink it, you'll think of Cuba and our culture.

*¡Salud!*

—*Emilio*

CUBA LIBRE

# Cuba Libre

### (RUM AND COKE WITH LIME)

———◦◦◦———

Most stories about how the Cuba libre was invented agree that the very first one was mixed in 1900, shortly after the Spanish-American War.

The way the story goes, a U.S. Army captain walked into a Havana bar and asked for a mix of Bacardi rum and Coca-Cola with a lime wedge in it. Some soldiers nearby heard him and ordered it as well. Soon enough they all got a little happy and, in the spirit of the times, shouted toasts of "¡Por Cuba libre!" which means "To a free Cuba!"

The toast became the name, and the name stuck. Without the lime, it's just a rum and Coke. The lime is what gives it a distinctively Cuban taste, different from the original. It's a truly tropical touch that brings out the best in Cuban rum and the sweetness of the soda.

You can also make it in a low-cal version by using diet soda in place of regular. Either way, remember to give at least one toast: ¡Por Cuba libre!

—Gloria

———◦◦◦———

**YIELD: 2 DRINKS**

| | |
|---|---|
| 4 oz light rum | ice |
| Coca-Cola | 2 lime wedges |

1. Fill two 12-ounce highball glasses with ice. Pour 2 ounces of light rum into each glass, fill to the top with coke, and garnish with a lime wedge.

### Tip from the Kitchen

For a lower-calorie version of this cocktail, use diet soda instead.

MOJITO DE MELÓN, MOJITO DE PIÑA,
MOJITO DE MANZANA, MOJITO DE MANGO
Y MOJITO TRADICIONAL

# Mojito

⸺◦⸺

The mojito is one of Cuba's most popular rum drinks. It is refreshing and potent.

Variations date back to the time of pirates who sailed in Cuba's waters, but the one we drink today was born in the 1930s in Havana, about the time Ernest Hemingway was living, fishing, and writing there.

The mojito depends on three very distinct Cuban ingredients: rum, lime, and sugar. The sugar is first mixed with warm water to make syrup, then add some freshly crushed mint, ice, and a splash of club soda, and you've got a drink that's distinctly Cuban.

By adding slices of fruit or flavored rums, it's easy to make variations on the original with a subtle touch of your favorite fruit flavor.

—Emilio

⸺◦⸺

# Mojito

## (CLASSIC MOJITO)

### YIELD: 2 DRINKS

1 lime, quartered

1 oz simple syrup (recipe below)

12 fresh mint leaves

ice

4 oz light rum

2 oz club soda

2 fresh mint sprigs

1. Take two 12-ounce Gibraltar glasses and place ½ of the lime, ½ oz of the simple syrup, and 6 mint leaves in each glass. Muddle to allow the mint leaves to release their oil and fragrance.

2. Add about a cup of ice and 2 ounces of rum to each glass. Then cover each with a cocktail shaker and shake well.

3. Remove the cocktail shaker, and top each drink off with a splash (about an ounce) of club soda.

4. Garnish each glass with a mint sprig and enjoy.

### Tip from the Kitchen

To make simple syrup, take equal parts of sugar and water, and combine in a microwave-safe bowl. Heat the mixture in the microwave for 2 to 3 minutes, stirring occasionally, until the sugar is completely dissolved. Let cool. Make as much simple syrup as necessary based on the number of drinks you plan to make.

# Mojito de Manzana

(SOUR APPLE MOJITO)

**YIELD: 2 DRINKS**

1 lime, quartered

1 oz simple syrup

12 fresh mint leaves

ice

4 oz sour-apple-flavored rum

2 oz club soda

Granny Smith apple wedges (or fresh mint sprigs)

1. Take two 12-ounce Gibraltar glasses and place ½ of the lime, ½ oz of the simple syrup, and 6 mint leaves in each glass. Muddle to allow the mint leaves to release their oil and fragrance.

2. Add about a cup of ice and 2 ounces of the sour-apple-flavored rum to each glass. Then cover each with a cocktail shaker and shake well.

3. Remove the cocktail shaker, and top each drink off with a splash (about an ounce) of club soda.

4. Garnish each glass with an apple wedge or fresh mint sprig and enjoy.

## Tip from the Kitchen

To prevent apple slices from turning brown, immediately after cutting the apples, place them in a bowl and sprinkle lemon juice all over the apple flesh.

# Mojito de Melón

(WATERMELON MOJITO)

**YIELD: 2 DRINKS**

1 lime, quartered

1 oz simple syrup

12 fresh mint leaves

ice

4 oz watermelon-flavored rum

2 oz club soda

watermelon wedges or fresh mint sprigs

1. Take two 12-ounce Gibraltar glasses and place ½ of the lime, ½ oz of the simple syrup, and 6 mint leaves in each glass. Muddle to allow the mint leaves to release their oil and fragrance.

2. Add about a cup of ice and 2 ounces of the watermelon-flavored rum to each glass. Then cover each with a cocktail shaker and shake well.

3. Remove the cocktail shaker, and top each drink off with a splash (about an ounce) of club soda.

4. Garnish each glass with a slice of watermelon or fresh mint sprig and enjoy.

# Mojito de Piña

(PINEAPPLE MOJITO)

**YIELD: 2 DRINKS**

| | |
|---|---|
| 1 lime, quartered | 4 oz pineapple-flavored rum |
| 1 oz simple syrup | 2 oz club soda |
| 12 fresh mint leaves | 2 oz pineapple juice |
| ice | pineapple wedges or fresh mint sprig |

1. Take two 12-ounce Gibraltar glasses and place ½ of the lime, ½ oz of the simple syrup, and 6 mint leaves in each glass. Muddle to allow the mint leaves to release their oil and fragrance.

2. Add about a cup of ice and 2 ounces of the pineapple-flavored rum to each glass. Then cover each with a cocktail shaker and shake well.

3. Remove the cocktail shaker, and top each drink off with a splash (about an ounce) of club soda and a splash (about an once) of pineapple juice.

4. Garnish each glass with a pineapple wedge or fresh mint sprig and enjoy.

# Mojito de Mango

(MANGO MOJITO)

**YIELD: 2 DRINKS**

| | |
|---|---|
| 1 lime, quartered | 4 oz mango-flavored rum |
| 1 oz simple syrup | 2 oz club soda |
| 12 fresh mint leaves | 2 oz mango juice or nectar |
| ice | fresh mint sprigs |

1. Take two 12-ounce Gibraltar glasses and place ½ of the lime, ½ oz of the simple syrup, and 6 mint leaves in each glass. Muddle to allow the mint leaves to release their oil and fragrance.

2. Add about a cup of ice and 2 ounces of the mango-flavored rum to each glass. Then cover each with a cocktail shaker and shake well.

3. Remove the cocktail shaker, and top each drink off with a splash (about an ounce) of club soda and a splash (about an once) of mango juice.

4. Garnish each glass with a fresh mint sprig and enjoy.

# Sangría

———— ∞ ————

Sangría is derived from a red wine punch that people drank in Europe for hundreds of years before Columbus made his famous voyage across the Atlantic.
The sangría of today was invented in Spain using rioja and other Spanish red wines. When the first Spanish settlers moved to Cuba, they carried the tradition with them. Over time, the recipe has evolved to include variations with locally available fruits just about everywhere it's warm—and plenty of places where it's not.

Ours blends the citrusy sweetness of orange juice and triple sec with red wine and a touch of club soda. Orange wedges and fruit cocktail add subtle hints of flavor and variety to the blend.

—Gloria

———— ∞ ————

**YIELD: 4 TO 6 DRINKS**

1 cup orange juice

2 oz triple sec

1 cup vodka

4 oz club soda or lemon-lime soda

1 cup fruit cocktail

2 cups ice

2 cups dry red wine

orange slices

1. Pour the orange juice, triple sec, vodka, and club soda or lemon-lime soda into a large pitcher. Add the fruit cocktail, ice, and red wine, and stir well.

2. Serve in red wine glasses and garnish with orange slices.

DAIQUIRÍ TRADICIONAL

# Daiquirí Tradicional

## (TRADITIONAL DAIQUIRI)

⸎

Y ou can thank an American mining engineer for the creation of one of Cuba's most well-known drinks.

Supposedly, somewhere around 1905, Jennings Cox was entertaining a group of guests in Santiago, Cuba, and he ran out of gin. So he grabbed a bottle of rum and mixed some drinks with sugar and lime juice over cracked ice. The name comes from the name of a nearby beach.

However it was invented, the daiquirí soon spread to the United States and exploded in popularity, especially during World War II when whiskey, vodka, and other liquors were rationed, but rum was readily available.

Several variations of the daiquirí have evolved over time, including flavored and "frozen" smoothie-style versions, but ours is the original, traditional recipe.

And you don't have to wait until you run out of gin to try it.

—Emilio

⸎

### YIELD: 2 DRINKS

4 oz light rum

4 oz lime juice or lemon juice

2 tsp sugar

ice

lime rinds or lemon rinds

1. Mix all the ingredients in a cocktail shaker with ice and strain into a chilled cocktail glass.

2. Garnish with lime rind or lemon rind.

# Batido

————⦿————

Batidos *are traditional Cuban milk shakes.*

*You can make* batidos *with just about any kind of fruit, but we base ours on the pungent and potent varieties that grow on the island—like papaya, mamey, mango, and guanabana. Others work just as well, but the rich, exotic flavors of Cuban fruits give our* batidos *a distinctive taste. Cuban-style milk shakes are thick and cool, refreshing and invigorating.*

*A truly unique Cuban milk shake is the* batido de trigo. *There's no fruit in it, just puffed wheat. That may sound odd to others, but this is puffed wheat like the kind they use in cereals. The shake comes out sweet and thick and very filling. Try it; you will be surprised at how good it really is.*

—*Emilio*

————⦿————

BATIDO DE MAMEY

# Batido de Mamey

(MAMEY [PRONOUNCED *MAH-MAY*] SHAKE)

**YIELD: 2 SERVINGS**

1 cup fresh mamey, peeled and cut into chunks

2 cups milk

4 tbsp granulated sugar or extra-fine sugar

1 to 2 cups ice, as desired

1. Place all the ingredients except the ice in a blender, and blend as you would a milk shake or smoothie. Add ice as desired and blend until smooth.

2. Serve and enjoy!

**Tip from the Kitchen**

You may use frozen mamey pulp if fresh mamey is unavailable or not in season.

# Batido de Papaya

(PAPAYA SHAKE)

**YIELD: 2 SERVINGS**

1 cup fresh papaya, peeled and cut into chunks

2 cups milk

4 tbsp granulated sugar or extra-fine sugar

1 to 2 cups ice, as desired

1. Place all the ingredients except the ice in a blender, and blend as you would a milk shake or smoothie. Add ice as desired and blend until smooth.

2. Serve and enjoy!

**Tip from the Kitchen**

You may use frozen papaya pulp if fresh papaya is unavailable or not in season.

BATIDO DE TRIGO

# Batido de Trigo

**YIELD: 2 SERVINGS**

**2 cups unsweetened puffed wheat**

**2 cups milk**

**4 tbsp granulated sugar or extra-fine sugar**

**1 to 2 cups ice, as desired**

1. Place all the ingredients except the ice in a blender, and blend as you would a milk shake or smoothie. Add ice as desired and blend until smooth.

2. Serve and enjoy!

# Café Cubano, Cortadito
# y Café con Leche

‑‑‑‑⋘⋙‑‑‑‑

W e Cubans take our coffee seriously; in fact, it's hard to imagine a day without it.

There is nothing more Cuban than café cubano. We start our mornings with it, end our meals with it, and shoot down jolts throughout the day. Our children get accustomed to dipping their pacifiers in the sugary foam of it from the time that they're toddlers. And a typical Cuban breakfast is to take freshly baked Cuban bread, slather the long slices with butter, and dip the hunks in a sweet blend of milk and coffee we call café con leche, the same way Americans might dunk a doughnut.

Some prefer a cortadito, a thick and sweet mix of evaporated milk and coffee. I like the original—a tiny shot, straight up, with some sugar. I can't begin the day without it.

However you like it best, café cubano will give you a true taste of our traditions.

—Emilio

‑‑‑‑⋘⋙‑‑‑‑

# Café Cubano

(CUBAN COFFEE)

YIELD: 6 SERVINGS

**dark-roasted coffee (espresso ground)**
**water**

**3 tbsp granulated sugar**

1. Fill the lower chamber of a 6-cup stove-top espresso maker with water. Fill the filter with the dark-roasted coffee. (The chamber should be well packed, so use a spoon or measuring cup to compress.)

2. Attach the upper chamber in accordance with manufacturer's instructions—it should be a snug fit.

3. Place sugar into a glass measuring cup with a capacity of at least 2 cups.

4. Place the espresso maker on the stove on medium heat and raise the lid. You will need to remain next to the stove for the next 4 to 5 minutes to watch for the first droplets of coffee to brew.

5. As soon as coffee droplets start to come into the upper chamber, pour a very small amount of this "first" coffee into the sugar, return the espresso maker to the stove, and reduce the heat to low.

6. Beat the sugar and coffee with a spoon vigorously until you achieve a thick, frothy paste. If you poured too much coffee into the measuring cup, it will be impossible to achieve the desired consistency, so remove some of the "wet" sugar (about 1 tablespoon at a time) and add additional granulated sugar (about 1 tablespoon at a time).

7. Once the coffee has completely brewed, pour into the sugar paste and stir gently with a spoon until the sugar foam has completely risen to the top.

8. Pour a shot (about 1½ ounces per shot) of coffee into 6 espresso cups and serve hot.

# Cortadito

(CUBAN COFFEE "CUT" WITH MILK)

YIELD: 6 TO 8 SERVINGS

**café cubano (see recipe above)**          **1 12-oz can evaporated milk**

1. While the coffee is brewing, heat 1 can of evaporated milk in a medium sauce-pan over low heat. Stay near the stove to make sure the milk doesn't scald or boil over.

2. Remove the saucepan from the heat as soon as the milk reaches a boil.

3. Using a sieve, strain 1½ to 2 ounces of the heated milk into each of 6 to 8 demitasse cups.

4. Top off with a shot of coffee so that you have about equal parts of evaporated milk and coffee.

5. Stir gently and serve hot.

# Café con Leche

(CUBAN-STYLE LATTE)

**YIELD: 6 SERVINGS**

*café cubano* **(see recipe above)**          **sugar, to taste**

**6 cups whole milk**

1. While the coffee is brewing, heat 6 cups of whole milk in a medium to large saucepan over low heat. Stay near the stove to make sure the milk doesn't scald or boil over.

2. Remove the saucepan from the heat as soon as the milk reaches a boil.

3. Using a sieve, strain about 1 cup of the heated milk into each of 6 coffee mugs.

4. Top off with a shot of *café cubano*.

5. Stir gently and serve hot. Add additional sugar, to taste.

# Acknowledgments

———∞∞———

WE WISH TO thank everyone at Penguin and Estefan Enterprises who made this book possible, as well as our loyal fans who motivate us to continue writing and creating. There are certain people whose love of our culture and of Cuban cuisine was a key ingredient in bringing this cookbook to life:

Gio Alma                Raymond Garcia          Mark Morales

Frank Amadeo            Roberto Gonzalez, Jr.    Moris Moreno

Ricardo Dopico         Leyla Leeming            David Rodriguez

Caridad De Diego       Miriam Peña              Kim Suarez

Gloria Fajardo         Christian Marin          Mauricio Zeilic

But most important, we wish to honor our parents and grandparents for sacrificing their dreams so that we could pursue ours.

—Emilio and Gloria Estefan

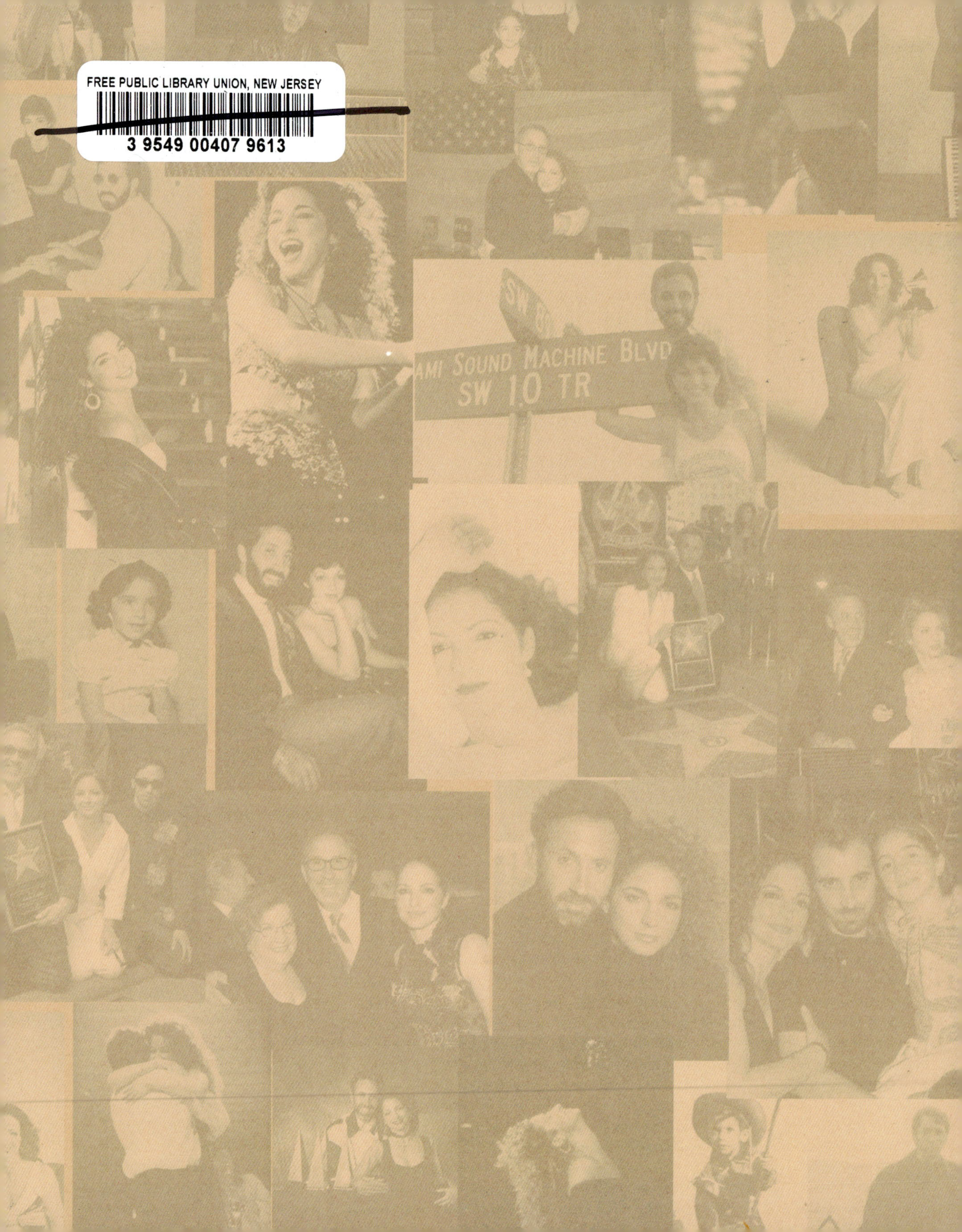
AMI SOUND MACHINE BLVD
SW 1 0 TR